A Judge and a Rope

I·O·W·A
HERITAGE
COLLECTION

IN IOWA?—THEN WHERE NOT?

A Judge and a Rope

and Other Stories of Bygone Iowa

by **GEORGE MILLS**

Iowa State University Press / Ames

GEORGE MILLS, longtime *Des Moines Register* staff writer and reporter for WHO-TV (Des Moines), is also the author of *Rogues and Heroes from Iowa's Amazing Past, The Little Man with the Long Shadow,* and *Looking in Windows: Surprising Stories of Old Des Moines,* also published by Iowa State University Press.

Frontispiece by **J. N. (Ding) Darling.** Reprinted by permission of the *Des Moines Register.* Illustrations that appeared originally in the *Des Moines Register* are reprinted here with permission of the *Des Moines Register.*

© 1994 Iowa State University Press, Ames, Iowa 50014

⊗ Printed on acid-free paper in the United States of America

First edition, 1994

Library of Congress Cataloging-in-Publication Data

Mills, George
    A judge and a rope and other stories of bygone Iowa / by George Mills. — 1st ed.
        p.   cm.
    ISBN 0-8138-0693-3 (alk. paper)
    1. Iowa—History—Anecdotes.   I. Title.   II. Title: Judge and a rope.
F621.6.M55   1994
977.7—dc20   94-27078

Contents

Foreword

F our generations of the George Mills family converged on the author's southside Des Moines home this spring to celebrate his eighty-eighth birthday. A few days after the family reunion, Mr. Mills phoned me to apologize that the birthday celebration had delayed his putting the finishing touches on *A Judge and a Rope,* his new book of Iowa history.

I smiled. This was the rare occasion when he would keep *me* waiting rather than the other way around. The fact is, George Mills still moves with the dispatch of a seasoned reporter covering a beat, one eye on the keyboard, the other on the clock. Though officially "retired" from the *Des Moines Register* for more than twenty years now, you will still see his byline regularly on the *Register*'s op-ed page, adding historical perspective to the front page's late-breaking development.

It's that extensive experience, stretching now across the larger part of the twentieth century, that makes the historical writing of George Mills appealing to so many readers. His storytelling ability is certainly unusual among contemporary historians, but so too is the precise fact-finding, a hallmark of the best watchdog political reporters, that informs his narratives. From his superb writing in previous publications such as *Rogues and Heroes from Iowa's Amazing Past, The Little Man with the Long Shadow,* and *Looking in Windows,* generations of Iowans have learned their state's history.

Like several of these earlier works, *A Judge and a Rope* contains character sketches as well as re-creations of dramatic incidents in Iowa history based on eyewitness accounts and recollections of the participants. In this new book, we encounter some familiar faces and several newcomers to the annals of Iowa history. There is the abolitionist firebrand, John Brown, who recruited several young Iowans for his bizarre attempt to capture the federal arsenal at Harpers Ferry in 1859. Brown's more moderate contemporary, William Seward, is seen here campaigning for Abraham Lincoln in Iowa the following year. And in a fine story about post–Civil War politics, we learn how Iowa City's Peter Dey helped put the brakes on the scandalous machinations of the Credit Mobilier, whose exploits disgraced the Republican administration in Washington.

There is more in *A Judge and a Rope* on the twentieth century than on the nineteenth, and here we have the benefit of the author's first-hand experience with the principals involved. In a story about a somewhat tarnished American hero, we eavesdrop on the disturbing speech delivered in Des Moines by aviator Charles Lindbergh, an apparent defender of European anti-Semitism in the early 1940s. By this time, Lindbergh was no longer the nation's boy wonder, and in any case Iowans had their own *wunderkind* in Henry A. Wallace—a charismatic gentleman, in equal parts scientist, businessman, and politician. In his home state Wallace was seen by many as the perennial Iowa boy next door, now serving valiantly in FDR's New Deal administration to help the nation's farmers regain control of their livelihood in the face of unprecedented economic and environmental hardships. Few profiles of Mr. Wallace are as insightful and moving as George Mills's "Cornfield Prophet," which appears here in print for the first time.

With his characteristic modesty, Mr. Mills would insist that these and the other essays in *A Judge and a Rope* just build on the work of earlier historians such as Benjamin Shambaugh, William Petersen, and Mildred Throne. But what readers treasure in Mr. Mills's writing is more than what he has learned from these past masters; it is how he has illuminated the meaning of all the names and the dates through compelling storytelling and striking characterizations. The *Register*'s Danny Katayama remarked on this in his 1990 review of *Looking in Windows,* paying tribute to Mr. Mills's "informal and relaxed way of passing on information." Readers will find the same lively style here in *A Judge and a Rope,* the latest offering by a man whose extensive experience has not diminished his fascination with the unpredictability of human behavior and the resilience of the human spirit.

BILL SILAG

Iowa State University Press
August 1994

Acknowledgments

I n addition to the author's recollections, this book is based on the following sources:

Newspapers: Principally the *Des Moines Register* and *Tribune* and their predecessors, *Iowa State Register, Des Moines Leader, Des Moines Capital* and *Des Moines News.* Also *Burlington Hawkeye-Gazette, Camp Dodge Dodger, Council Bluffs Nonpareil, Clinton Herald, Denison Bulletin and Review, Davenport Times, Eldora Herald-Ledger, Iowa City Republican, Le Mars Globe-Post, Le Mars Sentinel, Marshalltown Times-Republican, O'Brien County Bell, Orange City Journal, Sheldon Mail, Sioux City Journal,* and *Sioux City Tribune.*

Journals and reports: *Annals of Iowa, Iowa Journal of History and Politics, Palimpsest, Wallaces' Farmer,* 1969 Burroughs Clearing House report.

Personal conversations with Henry A. Wallace, Vice President and Secretary of Agriculture; President Harry Truman; John F. Kennedy (while a candidate for president); Governors Clyde L. Herring, Robert Blue and Herschel Loveless; Jake More, Mrs. Henry C. Wallace; Edward L. O'Connor, Iowa attorney general; Maj. Gen. Park Findley; Edith Johnson; Mrs. Warren Johnson; Jim Russell and Maurice Horner; Al Boss; Plymouth County Sheriff Ralph Rippey; Morris Cope; Martin Rosburg; Lawrence Krause; John Sokolovske; Rt. Rev. Msg. L.G. Ligutti; Bill Sentner; Floyd Page; Labor Commissioner Frank Wenig; Iowa legislators

Leo Hoegh, Earl Fishbaugh, Charles Van Eaton, George Paul, Gladys Nelson, Fred Schwengel, Clifford Strawman, J. Kendall Lynes, Phil Roan, Lawrence Putney, and House Speaker William Lynes. Also Flora Easter; Hanford MacNider; O.S. Von Krog; Percy A. Lainson; Fred Cooper; Elsie Woodley; Jane Maneely; Bonnie Jones; M.J. Greenfield; Wilbur Kenison; Lawrence Muhlenbruck; Merlin Numelin; Joe Liebendorfer, Hampton mayor; Dan Conley, Sioux City mayor; Evelyn Rice; Wayne E. Baker; Alvin P. Meyer; Leo Wegman, Iowa State Treasurer; Francis Cutler; Elmer Carlson; Ed Pillar; Kaare Mehl; Louise Bliesman; Robert De Jager; Flore Betti; Josie Velkie; Harry Pargas, and the guards at the entrance to the 1964 Democratic National Convention at Miami Beach, Fla. Also Mayo Buckner; Al Sasser; Mrs. Clarence Ver Steeg; Lee Swearengin; Carl Swearengin; Seth Perkins; Peter Baumann; Cloris Leachman; Hugh Moffett; Jacqueline Means; Bess Myerson; Joan Bunke; Don Harris; Edris Owens; Waldo Mead; Margaret Holthe; Ray Breen; C.P. Thompson; Frank Pierce; the Rev. Olaf Holen; the Rev. Allen Nelson; the Rev. Albert Abrahamson; and the Rev. George Blakesley.

Books: *Battle Flag Day,* published by the State of Iowa, 1896; *History of Iowa* by B.F. Gue, Century Co., New York, 1903; *Ioway to Iowa,* Irving B. Richman, State Historical Society of Iowa (SHSI), 1931; *I Remember, I Remember,* Cyrenus Cole, SHSI, 1936; *Iowa Through the Years,* Cyrenus Cole, SHSI, 1940; *Iowa: Its History and Its Foremost Citizens,* Johnson Brigham, S.J. Clarke Publishing Co., Chicago, 1915; *A Narrative History of the People of Iowa,* Edgar R. Harlan, American Historical Society, Chicago and New York, 1931; *A History of Iowa,* Leland Sage, Iowa State University Press, Ames, 1974; *Peter Anthony Dey,* Jack Johnson, SHSI, 1939; *William Boyd Allison,* Sage, SHSI, 1956; *Robert Gordon Cousins,* Jacob Swisher, SHSI, 1938; *John Brown and His Men,* Richard Hinton, Funk & Wagnalls, London and Ontario, 1894; *Who's Who In America;* and *Iowa Official Registers* (redbooks).

County histories: Des Moines, Dubuque, Marshall, Lee, Black Hawk, Grundy, Scott, and Marion.

Miscellaneous: Glenwood State School records; additional Lee Swearengin material given to the author after Lee's death; and Iowa State Dairy Association releases.

The author also wishes to express his appreciation for assistance provided by *Register* librarian Phyllis Wolfe and staff, and by the staffs of the Iowa law library and Iowa State Library.

A Judge and a Rope

There Was No Escaping

E xcitement shone on the faces of the whole Daniel Swearingen family.

Daniel, his wife Mary Ann, and the four children did not want to stop long in Nevada, Iowa. They had come from Ohio in a covered wagon pulled by horses. Now they were almost to the 160 acres in Webster County that was to be their home.

One or two more days!

Daniel and Mary Ann were in their early thirties. The children were Sarah Jane, 11, Rebecca Ann, 9, George, 7, and Sabrina, 2.

The travelers bought supplies in Nevada, including lard and cotton. The cotton was hung high in the schooner wagon.

"Giddyap!" shouted Daniel and the wagon moved out of Nevada toward Story City on the Fort Dodge road. A strong south wind was blowing. Tall brown grass rippled in long waves under the force of the moving air. Somewhere over the horizon lay the land where the Swearingens intended to build their home.

They never got there.

The time was November 1860. Outbreak of the Civil War was six months away. Many Iowa pioneers had concerns more pressing than a war that might never happen.

Prairie fires were a big worry that fall. Lush grass grew two to 10 feet tall. The grass was tinder dry that November. Roads to serve as windbreaks were few in the central Iowa countryside. Once a fire got going it might travel swiftly for miles. Some prudent farmers made their own firebreaks by plowing around their homesteads.

A prairie fire was a breathtaking spectacle—if you could ever forget its power to destroy human beings, crops, wildlife and sometimes homes. An 1859 Charles City newspaper said:

> Prairie fires are now raging in this vicinity. Each evening, as they are fanned by the night breezes, the flames blaze forth in every direction, lighting up the whole heavens with a lurid glare and giving them an aspect both beautiful and sublime.

A Story County report said:

> During high winds, the mighty flames would come at racehorse speed and sweep everything before them. It was a thrilling and awe-inspiring sight.

A Warren County pioneer reported:

> I have seen a fire go almost as fast as a horse could run. To see a prairie fire after night was one of the greatest sights; the whole prairie would be a burning mass.

In 1860 the fires were so bad in southwest Iowa that a stagecoach twice was turned back by flames between Clarinda and Bedford. In November 1861, fire raced 25 miles down the west side of the Des Moines River near Fort Dodge and stripped "nearly every farm of its fences."

More serious was the effect on farm operations. Haaver Thompson, northeast of Story City, had "practically nothing left except himself and his family" after fire swept through his place. A Mitchell County editor wrote after an autumn series of fires in 1856:

> We have heard of several farmers who have lost not only the entire fruits of their summer's labor but also their houses and stables, thus leaving them without shelter and their herds of cattle without fodder for the coming winter. This is a bitter pill for those who have to depend upon their daily toil. Houses can be rebuilt but the season is too far spent for hay gathering, even if the fire had made no ravages.

Most tragic were the fates of a little girl in Story County, a pioneer on East Lake Okoboji—and the six members of the Swearingen family.

Store Per, a Story County farmer, had a small daughter. The report on one fire in that county said:

The greedy flames sweeping westward did not spare Store Per's 7-year-old daughter who was caught in the furious onrush only a short distance from home, and burned to death. Per made every effort humanly possible but failed. What a trial to be visited upon the parents; what anguish, what sorrow!

A pioneer at East Okoboji told of seeing "a man burned to death before my very eyes—a terrible thing." The man had come west with his family to establish a home. When a prairie fire broke out, he put his family in a safe place near the lake. Then he walked back to see if the fire was out.

"Just as he reached the top of the hill," the pioneer wrote, "the fire came like the wind from below. The man turned and ran toward the area where his family waited. It was only a short distance and he ran as one who knew that death was reaching out for him. In the very sight of his children he ran and had almost reached them when the rolling flames overtook him. In an instant his hair and clothing were burning."

He staggered into the midst of his family and threw himself on the ground. They all fought the flames frantically. But it was too late. He died in a short time. He had breathed the flames and his lungs were burned.

In the case of the Swearingens, the wagon had traveled perhaps five or six miles when a prairie fire roared up from the rear. Daniel whipped the horses into a lumbering gallop down the crooked and rutty trail. But there was no escaping. It overtook the family in a little valley.

The wagon cover caught fire. Swearingen jumped down to the ground to battle the flames. He evidently stumbled. A frightened horse kicked him in the head. He was stunned into "partial insensibility." He revived in time to see the burned body of his wife fall from the wagon. He pulled the body of one child from the flames. The other three children were burned beyond recognition in the wagon. The frenzied Swearingen realized his whole family was dead. His eyesight about gone, he groped his way to a farm home a mile away.

"Here he was taken in and tenderly cared for," a report said, "but in spite of all that friendly hands could do, he expired from his burns."

$50 for a Hangman

S heriff John McKinney at Burlington was deeply bothered.

He had two young men to hang and he loathed doing it. He had to cut the rope that would spring the trap and send the victims to their deaths.

He could hear the wagons creaking by in the streets as thousands gathered to see the public executions on the edge of Burlington. Mississippi riverboats brought spectators from nearby Nauvoo, Illinois, and from as far away as Muscatine and Keokuk. The day was a clear and warm June 25 in 1845.

Here was the situation: John Miller, an old German, was murdered in his home on Devil Creek in Lee County. William and Stephen Hodges were arrested for the crime at Nauvoo, city of the Mormons.

A jury in the court of Judge Charles Mason in Burlington found both defendants guilty. The sentence: Death.

A small gallows was built on Mount Pleasant Street about 100 yards west of the Burlington Railroad tracks, in the valley of Hawkeye Creek.

Reports of the execution make chilling reading. Muffled drums and a dirge played by a brass band marked the slow progress of the lumber wagon carrying the prisoners to the gallows. One account says the young men were "shrouded and in chains" and sat astride their coffins on the wagon.

The people hurried to the scene to get good positions. Quite a few placed themselves near the gallows. Some parents allowed their children to witness the gruesome event. Boys climbed a nearby tree to get a good view.

"I was only a little girl then," one woman recalled. "Nearly everyone went and I was foolish enough to go, to my regret because it was two or three weeks before I could banish the horrible sight from my mind."

As they stood on the gallows, William Hodges remained silent. But Stephen said: "You are putting two innocent men to death. Hang us! We are Mormons!"

"An awful silence, still as death, pervaded the vast crowd covering vale and hill," said one account. "Sheriff McKinney, facing the crowd, called out: 'I will give any man $50 to cut this rope.'"

That was a lot of money in the 1840s. But nobody volunteered.

The reluctant sheriff picked up a hand ax, counted "once, twice, thrice," and severed the rope holding up the platform on which the two Hodges stood with ropes around their necks. The platform gave way.

One spectator said William died almost immediately of a broken neck. But the other side of the platform made an inclined plane down which Stephen's feet slid until the rope tightened. He died in agony of strangulation.

The bodies were taken to Nauvoo for burial.

Among those unhappy with the execution was Judge Mason. He could hardly bring himself to sign the death warrants. He called the hangings a "barbarous, uncivilized and unchristian code of punishment." He also was not certain the Hodges were guilty. The prosecutor, however, assured the judge that he had made "no mistake."

By Authority of God Almighty!

T he heart of Mother Coppoc was filled with foreboding. She tried desperately to keep her sons Edwin and Barclay at home in the Quaker village of Springdale, Iowa. She knew they planned to join abolitionist John Brown in a raid designed to start an insurrection among slaves in Virginia and Maryland. She was afraid she never would see the young men again.

She was partly right. Barclay was to return an emaciated fugitive. Edwin was to be hanged by the neck until dead by the state of Virginia for treason and murder.

The year was 1859. The nation was building up to the vast Civil War that would break out in two years, pitting the slave-holding South against the free-states North.

Edwin Coppoc was 24, Barclay 20. They fervently wanted to help end slavery. They started east in July. They said they were going to visit their boyhood home in Ohio. They didn't fool their mother.

They joined a small force, led by fiery Brown, converging on the town of Harpers Ferry, Va. A deep determination impelled the members. Like their leader, they felt they had instructions from God to attack slavery wherever it existed. They had utter confidence in Brown.

"Where he commanded, they marched without a murmur," said one writer. "Where he led, they hesitated not to follow. They fully realized that death was far more likely than success."

The Springdale area in eastern Iowa had been a training headquarters for Brown's little force. The men lived on the Maxon farm three miles from the village. There was a lot of affection at Springdale for Brown and his men, some of whom had been with him in his earlier bloody efforts to make Kansas an anti-slavery state. Said one writer:

> While the Quakers were opposed in principle to war, so warm were their sympathies for the oppressed that they found a way to hold in high esteem and admiration these fearless young men who had risked their lives in striking blows for freedom in Kansas.

But Springdale people were badly worried. They tried to talk Brown out of his grandiose plan to invade Virginia. Brown could not be swayed. After he left, one John Palmer shipped boxes of "carpenters tools" to the east from West Liberty, Iowa. The "tools" really were 196 rifles and as many revolvers that had been collected at Springdale.

All was quiet for several weeks. Then on Sunday night, Oct. 16, many residents of Harpers Ferry attended a frenzied religious revival. They were exhausted when it was over. They went home to bed. Across the Potomac River, John Brown prayed before putting on his old hat of the Kansas wars.

Leading a band of only 22, he crossed the Potomac bridge

into Harpers Ferry in a cold rain. The 17 white and five black attackers dashed into the federal arsenal and took possession. It was ridiculously easy. The arsenal contained 100,000 firearms and was guarded by only three watchmen.

The nation was astonished, bewildered and amazed at the bold action. Southern states were "convulsed with fear, rage and hate." Brown holed up, expecting slaves to rebel over a wide area and become a strong force for emancipation of all blacks.

Never was Brown more mistaken. Ignorant, uneducated and timid, the slaves did not spring to Brown's side. The cause was hopeless.

Brown had attacked eight days before he planned. He feared he had a traitor in his ranks. It may be that he had many more men signed up for the attack. One author says most of Brown's men had not yet arrived by Oct. 16. The attackers did free some slaves and imprisoned many more persons who appeared on the streets. When asked by what authority they had seized public property, the attackers replied, "By authority of God Almighty!"

BARCLAY COPPOC

Harpers Ferry residents didn't know what to do. Frustrated and upset, they streamed into saloons and proceeded to get drunk. Next morning was lively. A grocer fired at the attackers and was killed by return fire. Somebody firing from a second story window mortally wounded Brown's son Watson and killed another invader.

One hundred militia arrived at noon and spread out to command every escape route. The opposition

EDWIN COPPOC

grew by the hour. Brown's little force came under heavy fire. Oliver Brown, another of John's sons, was hit by a bullet. He went inside, quietly lay down, and died. The mayor of Harpers Ferry was killed. A Brown man carrying a flag of truce was mowed down by Virginia bullets.

An overwhelming attack on the armory forced Brown to retreat into the engine house. More militia poured into town. By nightfall Brown was down to three unwounded whites besides himself, and a few blacks. Outside were 1,500 foes.

The following night Col. Robert E. Lee, perhaps the greatest general of the upcoming Civil War, reached Harpers Ferry with 90 marines and two pieces of artillery. Brown remained calm and cool. One of his sons lay dead. Brown held a rifle in one hand while feeling with the other for life in the pulse of the second fatally wounded son.

At 7 o'clock Tuesday morning the marines charged. They broke into the engine house. One more defender was shot and two marines wounded. The situation had become too one-sided. Resistance ceased. In the charge, Brown was knocked down by a saber blow. A bayonet twice pierced his body.

Two Iowans died in that final charge. Steward Taylor, West Liberty wagon-maker, suffered a mortal wound while fighting bravely near the engine house. He lived his last three hours in agony. Jeremiah Anderson, a young Des Moines man who had studied for the ministry, was stabbed by three bayonets as he dropped his smoking gun. One report says he was pinned to a wall and left hanging. Another report says he was dragged outside where the angered crowd kicked his face and spat tobacco juice into his eyes. Others forced tobacco quids into his mouth. When he died in three hours, his body was jammed into a salt barrel.

One authority says that in the final attack Edwin Coppoc saw Robert E. Lee coming and took aim. Before Coppoc could fire, the report goes, a prisoner grabbed Coppoc's gun and saved Lee's life. It has been said that if Lee had been killed at Harpers Ferry, 100,000 Yankee lives might have been spared in the Civil War. Lee's brilliant leadership of the Confederate armies was a big reason why the South was able to keep the bloody war going for four years.

Ten of Brown's men were killed. Brown and six other members of his band were taken prisoner, Edwin Coppoc among them. Barclay Coppoc was not there. He had been assigned to guard duty across the river. He got away, as did several others. Barclay barely avoided capture in a merciless Virginia manhunt.

In a letter home from prison a few days afterwards, Edwin Coppoc wrote: "Whatever may be our fate, rest assured we shall not shame our companions by a shrinking fear. They lived and died like brave men. We I trust shall do the same."

And he did die a brave man on a Virginia gallows.

Here was the overall casualty toll: Brown's band, 10 killed, 7 executed; liberated slaves, 17 killed; citizens and soldiers, 8 killed, 9 wounded. Total deaths, 42.

Robust Politics

C annons boomed. Natty drill teams marched behind high-stepping bands. Rowdies threw rocks and eggs, and exchanged punches. Flaming torch parades lighted up towns at night. Big crowds listened to speeches that went on for hours.

The 1860 campaign for president was one of the noisiest and most exciting ever in Iowa. That was the political battle which led to Republican Abe Lincoln's first election to the nation's highest office. Old Abe defeated Stephen A. Douglas, the principal Democratic nominee, both nationally and in Iowa.

The pioneers loved the conflict and enthusiasm of that action-filled campaign.

A Cedar Valley Republican rally at Cedar Falls was one of the largest of the year. Uncounted thousands trooped in from Waterloo, Charles City, Waverly, Vinton and New Hartford as well as all over the northeastern Iowa countryside.

Two cannons named "the devil" and "the baby waker" were stationed at the head of Main Street in Cedar Falls.

Early in the morning the cannons roared an ear-splitting welcome for a Charles City band arriving in two crowded Conestoga wagons. The band had come 50 miles in two days to whoop it up musically for Lincoln. (Wagon travel on mud trails wasn't very fast in those days.) A Butler Center club brought an

American flag 18 feet long.

Thirty-three little girls dressed in white rode in the parade waving streamers saying: "Our fathers are for Lincoln." Three yoke of plodding oxen pulled a big flatboat carrying 100 young women wearing flower-printed hoop skirts. The Republican club of Cedar Falls sang this song:

> Abe Lincoln is our leader, of whom we all are proud;
> the tallest of our candidates, in the Presidential crowd;
> then huzza for freedom, huzza for liberty!
> Three cheers for Hamlin, for Lincoln three times three!

(Hamlin was the Republican candidate for vice president.)

At Keosauqua a Democratic rally drew a crowd of 7,000. Another 5,000 Democrats heard a speech at Indianola that lasted five hours.

Each party organized campaign clubs whose members marched incessantly. Democratic clubs were the "Hickories," the "Invincibles," the "Shirt-tail Rangers," and the "Little Giants." (Short-statured Douglas was called the "Little Giant.") Most colorful of the Republican clubs were the "Wide Awakes." Each Wide Awake wore a cap, a ribbon, and a cape and carried a torch. Officers carried colored lanterns.

The campaign got rough at times. The Wide Awakes of Knoxville and Montezuma journeyed to Pella to put on a parade. A Democratic rock thrown from the crowd conked a Wide Awake on the head.

A fight broke out. It is hard to tell exactly what happened. Newspaper accounts differ, depending on the politics of the editor. A Pella Republican paper said:

> While the "Wide Awakes" were parading our streets, quietly and in order, not disturbing anybody, a rock was thrown by some inhuman wretch, which hit a "Wide Awake" from Montezuma, inflicting a severe wound which bled all night.

The paper reported that the rock-thrower escaped. But another "Democratic scamp" was flushed with two rocks in his pocket. Republicans were cuffing him around when another Democrat jumped into the fray. The newcomer was also taking a beating when his son joined the battle and was "knocked on the head for his pains." The son started throwing rocks too. Then both father and son "made good use of their legs" and ran away.

Here's what a Democratic paper reported:

> The Knoxville "Wide Awakes" went down in a body and, soon becoming infuriated with bad liquor, commenced an unparalleled assault on the quiet Hollanders [of Pella]. One man had his eye gouged out and another was blinded. One little boy was accused of throwing rocks and was pounded by these brutes until nearly dead. His father attempted to rescue him but every few minutes he was obliged to lay down his child and fight over his senseless body. He at last got the boy to a doctor and dragged him in. . . . The atrocities were almost unparalleled in civil times.

CAMPAIGN POSTERS from the campaign of 1860.
Note the misspelling of Lincoln's first name.

It was the usual thing for zealots to go to an opposition party rally and cause all the trouble they could by throwing eggs. Three women, "one of them quite elderly," were hit by eggs at a Republican roundup in Bloomfield. Sharp-eyed Republicans "caught the miserable devil" with the eggs he did not have time to throw. He was roughed up good. Ruffians "yelling like Indians" disrupted the Republican meeting in Delaware Township, Polk County. Spectators "did everything that the basest malignity and the dirtiest blackguardism could suggest" to insult paraders at Agency.

It seems almost like sacrilege now, but the Iowa Democratic press gave the now-revered Lincoln a harsh going-over. One paper called him "this poor shell-bark politician from Illinois, a man of no culture or refinement, possessing no ability as a statesman." Another paper asked: "What Republican does not blush with shame at Old Abe's record?" Republican papers similarly scorched Douglas.

Meantime, a throng of 25,000 poured into Keokuk from southeast Iowa and Illinois for a huge Republican rally. At Fairfield a Republican parade was said to have been five miles long. The Fairfield crowd was so big that orators delivered speeches at three different places simultaneously.

One campaign tactic popular everywhere was "raising a pole." Both parties erected exceptionally tall flag poles in communities all over the state. The poles consisted of trunks of young trees spliced together. "The good Democratic yeomanry" of Story County raised a "splendid hickory pole" 146 feet high, a tremendous height for a flagpole any time. Atop, a Democratic flag "floated to the breeze."

But other poles as tall or taller soon appeared. Republicans put up one of 146 feet at Palmyra in Warren County. The party erected another of 150 feet at Bloomfield. Ottumwa Republicans thought they had won the race with a pole 200 feet high. But Eddyville Democrats raised "a splendid hickory pole" with a claimed height of 214 feet (only to have lightning lop 110 feet off the top.) Republicans charged "villainous rowdyism" when somebody cut down their tall pole in Des Moines.

A major concern of each side was to keep the other from stealing the election in Iowa.

A Democratic warning said the Republicans planned to bring

in a lot of Kansans to vote illegally:

> An infamous plot has been concocted to carry this state for
> Lincoln by the importation of some miserable lazzeroni which
> has infested Kansas for years. The proof is now clear and
> indisputable that they are to be quartered in sparsely settled
> districts of Iowa to assist in carrying the state against the
> Democracy. Let the smallest precinct be watched and every
> vote examined.

The Republicans in turn warned against the possibility of
Democrats stealing or destroying ballots: "The opposition in some
parts of the state is desperate. Be prepared for any emergency."

The 1860 speeches sometimes sounded recurring themes
reminiscent of the politics of today. Speaking in Dubuque for the
Republican cause, William Seward of New York said slavery
wouldn't have been profitable on Iowa farms.

> It thus enters into the elements of a great and prosperous state
> that its people shall not be slaves but free men. It is not wealth
> alone that makes a nation. It must have strength and power to
> command peace and good order at home and respect and
> confidence abroad. A nation to be great wants character,
> character for justice, honesty and integrity, ability to maintain
> its own rights and respect for the rights of others. That it can
> not have if it be a nation of slaves.

(Seward served as Secretary of State in the Lincoln cabinet.)

Lincoln didn't come to Iowa but Douglas did. He spoke at big
rallies in Dubuque and Iowa City. The turnout was estimated as
high as 15,000 to 20,000 at Dubuque. A parade from the railroad
depot took Douglas to the Julien House, then "up Fourth to
Locust and around again to Main to escape marching under a
Lincoln flag suspended across Main Street." Democrats called the
location of that flag a "studied insult." That night a torchlight
parade was said to have outshone similar Republican processions
"as a firefly by the side of the Milky Way."

In the Dubuque speech, Douglas defended the Southern
position on blacks:

> It may be entirely safe in Iowa, where you have very few
> Negroes, to give them rights and privileges which it would be

unsafe and dangerous to give them in South Carolina where the slaves outnumber the whites two to one. Hence, you must allow the people of South Carolina to manage their own affairs, regulate their own institutions, take care of their own Negroes and mind their own business, and they must let us alone.

Another report said that 20,000 persons jammed the grounds where Douglas spoke in Iowa City. There he had strong words for keeping the union intact.

"The Union can not be dissolved without severing ties that bind the heart of the daughter and the son to the father," Douglas said with considerable emotion. "The Union can not be dissolved without separating us from the graves of our ancestors. We can not permit this Union to be dissolved. It must be preserved."

As it turned out, Lincoln was elected only because of the major splits in the Democratic Party. His total national vote of 1,866,000 was nearly one million less than that of his combined opposition. Douglas polled 1,375,000; John C. Breckenridge, a former vice president (1857-1861) and candidate of southern Democrats, got 845,000; and John Bell, candidate of the Constitutional Union Party, 589,000.

Lincoln did win a clear majority in carrying Iowa. He polled 77,409 votes to 57,922 for the combined opposition. Douglas was second with 55,111. Breckenridge got only 1,763 and Bell 1,048.

It now doesn't seem right for anybody much to have voted against the revered Old Abe, but many Iowans obviously did. Douglas carried 25 counties, including Dubuque, Wapello, Lee by a little, and a number along the southern border such as Appanoose, Decatur, Wayne and Fremont. Dubuque went for Douglas, 3,058 to 2,091.

Lincoln captured 69 counties. His best over Douglas included Scott, with 2,737 to 1,379; Linn, 2,227 to 1,290; Henry, 2,148 to 1,065; Black Hawk, 1,122 to 551; Clayton, 2,089 to 1,571; Clinton, 1,972 to 1,450. Polk voted 1,304 to 1,075 for Lincoln.

The vote was tiny in a number of counties which had practically no population as yet. For example, Ida County total was four for Lincoln and six for Douglas. Buena Vista County gave six to each. Another tied county was Pottawattamie with 412 each.

Republicans wildly celebrated the Lincoln victory everywhere.

In Des Moines they built a huge bonfire at Court Avenue and Third Street and wound around the downtown area in a boisterous torchlight parade. They built a rail fence in the middle of a street in honor of Lincoln, whose popular nickname was "the rail-splitter" because of his legendary prowess with an axe.

Adding a somber touch to the victory celebrations was the worry of a possible impending breakup of the Union. A Grundy County convention countered that concern with an angry resolution declaring: "We will stay in the Union and we will make all others stay in it, or do as General [Andrew] Jackson would have done, hang all who attempt to get out of it."

It took four bloody years of the Civil War to force the south to return to the Union, and 13,000 Iowans lost their lives in that great struggle.

Wrecked National Convention

A n Iowan touched off a row that broke up a Democratic national convention. As a result, a Republican won the presidency.

The Iowan was Ben Samuels, Dubuque lawyer and Democratic delegate. The Republican president was Abraham Lincoln. It all happened in 1860.

What a field day television would have had with the Democratic convention (or conventions) that year! Announcers would have shouted with excitement in reporting the suspense, conflict and bitterness over the deepening split between delegates of the North and South over extension of slavery into territories that were not yet states. The Civil War was less than one year in the future.

At one point Samuels cried to the Southerners on the convention floor at Charleston, S.C.: "Oh gentlemen, I beseech you, as you love your country, as you respect your friends, fetter us not in this hour, for fetters are fatal to us!"

Samuels and other Northern delegates objected strenuously to a platform that recommended masters be permitted to take slaves into territories, whether the territories liked it or not.

(Kansas and Nebraska were still territories.) Owners wanted to take their property (slaves) wherever they pleased. Northern Democrats knew defeat was certain in the free states (including Iowa) with such a platform.

Samuels led the floor fight that defeated the slavery plank. He was interrupted 18 times by applause in his emotional speech. When the results were announced on the slavery-plank vote, delegates of seven Southern states walked out. Delegates of 26 other states remained. They balloted 17 times without succeeding in nominating a presidential candidate.

The Charleston convention adjourned and met again in a few weeks at Baltimore, Md. Another row. This time the dissension was so great that even the convention chairman walked out.

In the end two rival Democratic conventions each nominated its own candidate. They were Stephen A. Douglas of Illinois and John Breckenridge of Kentucky. Iowa's eight delegates supported Douglas all the way.

To make matters worse for the Democrats, a third major party put a candidate in the field. John Bell of Tennessee was named by the "Constitutional Union" Party.

With the opposition so divided, there was little doubt as to the outcome of the November election. Had the Democrats been able to unite behind one candidate, it is likely that the Lincoln legend never would have come into being.

Ben Samuels is a forgotten Iowan, and that's too bad. He was an able lawyer and topflight speaker. He was the Democratic nominee for governor of Iowa in 1857, losing to Republican Ralph Lowe of Keokuk.

Samuels has been described as "tall, athletic, smooth-shaven, with an oval face and brown hair." He frequently wore a "swallow-tail blue coat with brass buttons." Even his political opponents called him a "good fellow" and an "honorable man." That was a lot more respectful than the things rival politicians said and did in the sometimes nasty ensuing campaign of 1860.

Blood and Compassion

Thousands of wounded soldiers lay helpless in bloody clothes on the naked ground for days after the battle. The suffering and the stench became almost unendurable.

Into this aura of despair strode Ann Harlan of Mount Pleasant, Iowa. She brought a wonderful message: Some of the badly injured and sick were going home! Right away! A boat was waiting!

Ambulances hurried shattered men to the riverbank. Others were carried on stretchers by comrades. Still others crawled to that boat "on their hands and knees."

The stricken were casualties of Shiloh, a vast, murderous battle of the Civil War, fought April 6 and 7, 1862, near the Tennessee River in southwestern Tennessee. Nearly 3,500 men were killed in action in the two terrible days, 1,735 on the Union side and 1,728 on the Confederate. The wounded numbered a huge 15,984, of which 7,882 were Union and 8,012 were Confederate. In addition, the Union reported 3,956 missing, the Confederates 359.

Iowa regiments lost 235 killed and 999 wounded in the two days.

The Union armies of the North had staved off the South, but at what a cost!

When she heard the Shiloh news, Mrs. Harlan could not sit still in Washington. She was the wife of U.S. Senator James Harlan. She prevailed upon Secretary of War Edwin Stanton to give her a pass to visit the battlefield.

She traveled by train to St. Louis, where she had a steamboat loaded with supplies and medicines. Her route to Shiloh was up the Mississippi River to the Ohio and then up the Tennessee to Pittsburg Landing, a point close to the battle area.

She was only one of many to start for Shiloh. "Hundreds of fathers and mothers, wives and sisters and sons and brothers were hastening to this terrible scene of carnage, with hopes of rescuing their beloved ones wounded in that awful battle, or if too late for this, to secure their remains for decent burial."

Every southbound boat on the Mississippi "was crowded with these messengers of mercy." But they didn't get to Shiloh. All civilian boats were halted at Cairo, Ill. Union commanders did not want crowds of civilians on the battlefield. Not even Illinois Governor Richard Yates was permitted to proceed with a boat loaded with supplies for the wounded and sick of his state.

But General Henry Halleck, the Union commander-in-chief, gave in to Mrs. Harlan. Seeing her pass from Stanton, he said: "Madame, you outrank me. What are your commands?"

She requested, and got, not only authority to go to Shiloh but also to take ambulances and assistants to distribute food, medicine and clothing. When she left Cairo, Governor Yates went along on her boat, "a Governor of a sovereign state—under the protection of one of Iowa's daughters."

As she worked with the afflicted men, Mrs. Harlan concluded that their chances of surviving depended on their getting home quickly.

"She could not avoid the conviction that hundreds, perhaps thousands, would perish if retained in camp or field hospitals, [but] would rapidly recover their health and strength if sent to their respective states," said one account. "Hence, she endeavored to induce the medical authorities to permit her to remove the dangerously wounded and almost helplessly sick Iowa troops to their own state. This request was at first harshly refused."

The determined Mrs. Harlan again went to Halleck, who agreed to her request, provided she would also take men from other Midwest states on the boat. That was fine with her, and the *D.A. January* left for Keokuk, Iowa, with some 280 wounded and sick aboard, including approximately 60 Iowans. On the same boat to help with the work en route was Annie Wittenmyer of Keokuk, Iowa's most famous angel of mercy in the war.

The women worked aboard trying to help the suffering men as much as possible. But some died on the river journey.

Mrs. Harlan wired ahead requesting that Keokuk get ready for what was coming. Another boat, the *Empress,* also was bound for Keokuk at the same time with perhaps 250 more soldiers.

Keokuk authorities had no facilities available for such emergencies and had to take over the Estes House, a major hotel which was converted into a 650-bed hospital.

The *D.A. January* reached Keokuk two weeks after Shiloh. Thirty-nine of the men wanted to go to their homes "at once and seemed quite able to ride." But the story was sadly different for others. At least seven soldiers of the 15th Iowa regiment alone soon died in Keokuk. The 15th suffered 188 casualties at Shiloh, more than one-fourth of the regiment's total strength of 760 men. The seven who died were George H. Huhn, Albia; Aaron Clingman, Danville; H.G. Vincent, Calhoun; Israel Warner and C.L. Kirk, Hopewell; Levi Randolph, Knoxville; and Henry Elmer, Kilbourne. All died of wounds or amputations except Clingman, who was a victim of tuberculosis.

There were no such things as slight wounds in those days. Antibiotics and other modern medicines were unknown. Many died of wounds which today would inconvenience a soldier only a few weeks at the most.

The magnitude of the Keokuk hospital problem was demonstrated by a report that showed 7,396 military patients were cared for in that city by the end of 1863, of whom 617 died. A number of additional hospitals had to be established quickly to meet the need.

Shiloh was but one of Mrs. Harlan's contacts with the blood and horror of war. She did mercy work with the Army of the Potomac in Virginia, where she found all troops, well and sick, living almost exclusively on "hard bread, salt meat and coffee." Many suffered from diarrhea.

"They would fight with each other for possession of a stray potato, onion or turnip," she said, "and a slice of common, soft baker's bread was prized by them as a luxury."

Mrs. Harlan placed a notice in the Washington papers saying her waiting boat would carry to the troops in Virginia any item which "patriotic and humane people of the city" might want to donate. She said the soldiers above all wanted "soft baker's bread."

The boat departed with what was called a "shipload of baker's bread." Guards had to be posted around bread-carrying ambulances in the field to keep well soldiers from grabbing it all. And food was only part of the problem.

"I frequently found sick soldiers lying by the roadside, soldiers who had been creeping for three or four days in search of a hospital," she said, "with nothing to eat but common bacon and hard bread for themselves in their knapsacks, being [almost] totally destitute. In fact, coats, blankets and knapsacks were to be seen everywhere strewn along the roads, which had been abandoned by sick men too feeble to carry them."

Such information from his wife made Senator Harlan an

expert on the medical policies of the Union army. He used that knowledge to force improvements in "the efficiency of this branch of the service."

Mrs. Harlan also turned a critical spotlight on the various home front programs for helping the soldiers. The food and supplies sent to the army by the people at home were known as "sanitary goods." She found the "sanitary" program of other states much better run than that of Iowa. She said:

> There was no head to the Iowa system, no home office at which accounts could be kept, no business arrangement for the shipment of goods, [no] transportation and subsistence for those soldiers who were discharged and without funds to pay their expenses home.

She was concerned over the possibility of frauds. She was also impatient with the jealousies of "petty interests and the ambitions of individuals." She was instrumental in the calling of an "Iowa State Sanitary Convention," which met in Des Moines in 1863 and which approved a coordinated approach for handling all soldiers' aid.

There is little question but that Ann Harlan helped save many lives by her diligent work and her determination to correct faults in the systems that provided care for soldiers. But why did this woman, who moved in high society, become involved in such rough and tough activities? It was the common opinion then that ladies should stay home, that they had no business in the blood and dirt of battlefields.

Mrs. Harlan, however, was a sad person. She had recently lost "a lovely and beautiful daughter, Jessie Fremont Harlan." The care of troops seemed to have become an outlet for her motherly sorrow.

Was she motivated at all by the fact that her work might help her Senator-husband politically? Perhaps, although she doesn't seem to have tried to get a lot of publicity for the Harlan name. She mostly seems to have been self-effacing personally about it all. In a note to Iowa women in 1863, she said:

> My dear sisters in the holy cause, do not afflict me by entertaining the thought that I address you on account of any vain desire for notoriety. Nothing could be more painful to the

feeling of a true woman. Like you, I would prefer to work on, hereafter as heretofore, in silence and, as far as possible, unobserved.

She developed health problems about that time but she was able to continue the work in some degree until the war ended in 1865. She did not die until 1884. She was buried in Forest Home Cemetery in Mount Pleasant "by the side of her three departed children and with military honors."

Gang of Thieves

P eter Dey refused to be associated with a gang of thieves bent on looting the United States treasury. That's why he resigned in 1864 as chief engineer for construction of the Union Pacific Railroad in the pioneer West.

He thus got clear of the Credit Mobilier company, perpetrator of a great national scandal of the nineteenth century. Disclosure of corruption in building the railroad ruined Vice President Schuyler Colfax politically; damaged Henry Wilson, another vice president; tarnished James Garfield, later president; and cast a shadow over numerous members of Congress.

The Mobilier conspirators pocketed some $5 million in ill-gotten gains, perhaps equivalent to $50 million in modern inflated dollars.

The Union Pacific was built from Council Bluffs, Iowa, to Promontory, Utah. There it met the Central Pacific from San Francisco in 1869, giving the nation its first transcontinental rail service. Federal subsidies paid the construction costs—and then some in graft.

Credit Mobilier was a private company which let the construction contracts. There was no competitive bidding. The plan called for the chief engineer to estimate the costs and for the contracts to be based on his figures.

Peter Dey, who lived in Iowa City, estimated the cost at $30,000 a mile for building 247 miles in the Platte River valley in Nebraska.

The Mobilier promoters instructed him to raise the estimate

to $50,000 a mile. Why shouldn't he? After all, Washington was paying the bills.

Dey would not stand for larceny of $20,000 a mile. He quit. He regretfully observed that he was leaving "the best possible position in my profession this country has offered to any man." But he didn't want to have "my name connected" with such thievery.

The contract to build the 247 miles thereupon was let to Herbet H. (Hub) Hoxie of Des Moines for $50,000 a mile. Hoxie was a high-up Republican with strong railroad connections.

The Hoxie contract angered Dey. "No man," he declared, "can call $50,000 a mile up the Platte valley anything but a big swindle—and thus it will stand forever."

Congressman Oakes Ames of Massachusetts appears to have been a main cog in the conspiracy. He bribed other congressmen by enabling them to buy Credit Mobilier shares of stock at half their value.

Other Mobiliers included Oliver Ames, brother of Oakes and later governor of Massachusetts, and Thomas C. Durant, founder of the company. After an investigation, the U.S. House of Representatives issued a rebuke against Oakes Ames. His congressional career came to an end in 1873 when the furor was at its height.

In another instance, Peter Dey recommended that the Union Pacific follow a route of 17 miles between two points. Durant instead called for a route that raised the distance to 26 miles, or nine extra miles of unneeded and expensive construction in Dey's eyes. He said of Durant:

> If the geography were a little larger, I think he would order a survey around the moon and a few of the fixed stars, to see if he could not get more. It is like dancing with a whirlwind to have anything to do with him.

Dey had been chief engineer in the early 1850s for construction of the old Rock Island line in Illinois. That was when he hired the later-famous Grenville Dodge of Council Bluffs as his assistant. In 1853 Dey surveyed across Iowa the route of the proposed Mississippi & Missouri Railroad, which became part of the Rock Island system. Again Dodge was his assistant.

Dey, who later served as mayor of Iowa City, was held in high regard. One writer said: "He dealt in facts only. I think the only question he ever asked himself was: 'Is it right?' In the university city, he was more than a man; he was an institution." Dey long was a major member of the Iowa State Railroad Commission and president of the First National Bank of Iowa City.

Grenville Dodge is notable in history as one of the top Union generals in the Civil War. After the war he took over as chief engineer for building the Union Pacific. He is generally credited with having done an outstanding job.

Dodge was not above illegal dealings, however. He was up to his ears in the scandal over location of the Iowa Statehouse on Des Moines' east side in 1857. But whether he got himself involved in Credit Mobilier was never learned. One writer said Dodge may have done what he could to satisfy the promoters "without selling his soul to Mephistopheles."

Of all the men Dodge ever knew, he held Union General Ulysses S. Grant and Peter Dey in the greatest respect. When Dodge laid out the city of Cheyenne, Wyoming (in connection with the Union Pacific project), he named one of the streets Dey Street. He wrote of Dey: "I look back on my services with him with the greatest pleasure." The general was shaken when Dey died in 1911.

Herbert Hoxie seems to have avoided special attention in the Mobilier probe even though he had won the questionable $50,000-a-mile contract. He is feted in history as a big time early Republican and a major railroad builder and promoter.

Hoxie was among the many Republicans who descended in force on

PETER A. DEY
Courtesy of the State Historical Society

Washington looking for jobs after Lincoln's election as president in 1860. Hoxie was named United States marshal for Iowa, a prestigious post. He was general manager of the Missouri Pacific Railroad at the time of his death at 56 years of age in 1886.

Two special trains brought railroad luminaries from around the Midwest to the Hoxie funeral in Des Moines. Dozens of big names in the industry were present at the graveside ceremonies in Woodland Cemetery, Dodge among them.

A Rambunctious Wedding

L est you think Iowa pioneers were all solemn, prim, stick-in-the-mud people, take a look at this story related by a guest at a rambunctious 1873 wedding at Neola in western Iowa:

> Last night a party drove up, assembled in the parlor of the hotel and sent for the landlord. They had come in from the prairie and were in search of an official to tie the knot that would make a couple one and inseparable forever more.
>
> I was invited to witness the ceremony and, ascending to the parlor, found the expectant bridegroom, a man about 40 years of age, and a fair and blushing damsel of sweet 16, awaiting impatiently the arrival of the parson. For some reason, no preacher could be found, and they were obliged to fall back on a young fellow, a newly elected Justice of the Peace who had never before officiated at a ceremony of this kind.
>
> He was very nervous at the idea of having to perform the ceremony and brought with him a copy of "Every Man His Own Lawyer," through which he looked for the desired form. Not finding any, and the crowd growing impatient, he told the couple to stand up and hold up their right hands. This done, he pronounced the following charge:
>
>> You and each of you do solemnly swear that in the cause now upon hearing, you will tell the truth, the

whole truth and nothing but the truth, and that you
will love, honor, cherish and obey each other
during the term of your natural lives, so help you
God.

Both answered solemnly, "I will." Then the Justice
charged them a dollar each and pronounced them man
and wife. One of the friends then produced a jug of
whisky from their sleigh and proceeded to compound a
punch, of which the whole party drank freely, and then
had a dance.

As they could find no music, their efforts were
confined principally to jigs and breakdowns. At last the
party concluded to put the happy couple to bed. The
bride was willing to go because she said she was tired
and her shoes pinched her feet. The girls of the party
took her off to her chamber and soon disrobed her and
announced to the young men that everything was ready.

All repaired to the bridal chamber where the face of
the new made bride was sweetly reposing on the pillow.
After perpetration of the customary jokes, the young
fellows intimated to the bridegroom that they proposed
to divest him of his wearing apparel and put him by the
side of his wife.

He objected and a scuffle ensued. The bridegroom
was as strong as an ox and, getting angry, he blackened
one fellow's eye and tore another one's coat off his back.
In the turmoil, the whole party got out of the room and
went to a saloon close by and took a drink.

In spite of all persuasions, the newly married man
declared that he was not going to let them take off his
clothes. His friends then got a rope and, making a noose,
slipped it over his head and tried to drag him upstairs.
They nearly choked him to death, when a doctor
interfered and cut the rope.

Then they fastened it to his legs and, in trying to
drag him upstairs, broke a lounge and tore down half the
bannister. Finding they could not get him upstairs, they
went up to see if they could not make the bride get up
and come down. But she had locked the door and would

not let the crowd in.

Some of them got a hammer and nails and, getting a ladder, put it on the outside of the house, climbed into the bride's apartment and nailed up the door, saying that if the bridegroom would not let them put him to bed, he should not get into the room anyhow.

They hid the ladder and went off. The happy man, finding the way clear, walked quietly up to his room and attempted to enter. He could not get in and he shouted, "My dear, open the door." She informed him it was nailed up. He then tried to kick it open when the landlord interfered and told him he was not going to have furniture and his house ruined in that way.

He [the bridegroom] went out and tried to find the ladder but could not do it. At last someone remembered that a lightning rod man had some ladders at the other barn, and so down the newly married man hastened. He secured a ladder, and at half past five in the morning he succeeded in joining his bride in the room above.

This morning the party returned home, declaring that they had the jolliest wedding ever known in Neola.

Tennis Net

W hen Abraham Lincoln departed from Mount Pleasant, Iowa, he left a tennis net with a friend to keep until his return.

But he never returned.

He died in London, England, on March 5, 1890, at only 16 years of age. The net is still in Mount Pleasant.

This Abraham Lincoln was the namesake and only grandson of the great Civil War president. The boy's other grandfather was U.S. Senator James Harlan of Mount Pleasant.

The Lincoln-Harlan tradition always has been reverent and strong in Mount Pleasant.

President Lincoln appointed his friend Senator Harlan to the Cabinet post of Secretary of the Interior in 1865. The senator had escorted Mrs. Lincoln at the president's second inaugural in 1864. The Lincolns and Harlans sometimes went out driving together around Washington.

Harlan came to the bedside when Lincoln was dying from an assassin's bullet in 1865.

In 1868 Robert Todd Lincoln married Mary Harlan. Robert was the only Lincoln child to reach maturity. Similarly, Mary was the only Harlan child to reach adulthood.

The Robert Lincolns were the parents of young Abraham, who was known as "Jack," and two daughters.

Robert Lincoln, a dignified and austere person, was president of the Pullman Company in Chicago. His family spent much time at the Harlan home in Mount Pleasant, particularly in the summertime. The Lincoln children were well liked by the Mount Pleasant younger set.

Abraham, or Jack, was described as "a handsome, gentlemanly boy, with charming manners."

"His favorite sport was tennis and when he left with his family for England, after his father was appointed United States minister to Great Britain, his tennis net was left in the care of a Mount Pleasant friend."

Young Abraham went to France to learn the French language preparatory to entering Harvard. He became ill of a carbuncle. He underwent a series of operations. After 17 weeks, the boy was brought back to London, where he died. His death ended the last hope of direct survival of the Lincoln name through the president's descendants.

The tennis net is part of the historic collection of Iowa Wesleyan College in Mount Pleasant. Also in the collection is a closet door on which Grandfather Harlan recorded with pencil marks the heights of the three Lincoln-Harlan grandchildren. Harlan was an early Iowa Wesleyan president and longtime trustee.

The last three Lincoln descendants, all children of Robert Lincoln's daughters, were Lincoln Isham of New York, Mary Lincoln Beckwith of Vermont and Robert Todd Lincoln Beckwith of Washington. None had children of their own. With their deaths many years ago, the Lincoln line became extinct.

Mary Lincoln Beckwith, who never married, was born in Mount Pleasant. Her mother, Jessie, eloped in 1897 with Warren

W. Beckwith of Mount Pleasant. Beckwith was an Iowa Wesleyan athlete.

Robert Todd Lincoln was an astute Chicago businessman. He inherited $110,000 from his parents and built up a sizable fortune. He died in 1926. The estate was valued at upwards of $3 million back in the 1950s. After the deaths of the great-grandchildren, the estate was divided three ways, one-third to Iowa Wesleyan, one-third to the American Red Cross and one-third to the Christian Science Church.

It was on April 11, 1865, that President Lincoln made what proved to be his last public appearance, and Iowa's Senator Harlan was the only other speaker. The South had surrendered to end the Civil War. A happy crowd gathered at the White House that evening and shouted for Lincoln.

The president appeared at a window and talked briefly about how the conquered Confederates should be treated (his "malice toward none" philosophy). Lincoln then introduced Harlan, who said the war had established these principles: That "majority should rule and no part of the republic should ever be permitted to secede."

Three nights later President Lincoln was shot and fatally wounded at Ford's Theater in Washington.

Battle Flag Day

"If any man attempt to haul down the American flag, shoot him on the spot!"

That defiant message appeared in big letters on an arch over Locust Street in downtown Des Moines. The occasion was "Battle Flag Day," August 10, 1894. Approximately 5,000 Iowa Civil War veterans came to town to march for the last time behind their regimental banners of the 1861-1865 war.

The banners had been stored for nearly 30 years in the old state arsenal at Locust and First streets, the present location of the Y.M.C.A. What the veterans did was parade their faded and torn colors up to the Statehouse. There the banners still may be seen in crumbly condition in display cases in the rotunda.

There were plenty of American flags as well in that mile-long march. Needless to say, nobody hauled down an American flag that day, or burned one either.

Large crowds lining the streets were hushed. The people were too moved to cheer the marchers. Rarely has Iowa witnessed a scene so filled with emotion. The state sent close to 76,000 men into the bloody Civil War and 13,000 died. That toll was almost as large as the combined deaths of Iowans in all the nation's wars since, including the Spanish-American War, both world wars, the Korean War, the Vietnam conflict and "Desert Storm." And Iowa had less than 25 percent of 1990's population when the Civil War broke out.

The Civil War is remote history to nearly all Iowans now. The state's last veteran of that war died in 1949. But that conflict with its pride and sorrows still was fresh in the memories of many who watched the 1894 parade.

"None cheered—their hearts were stirred too deep," said one account. "The tinge of melancholy that seized upon the multitudes almost silenced demonstration—the occasion was too great for noise. There were white-haired mothers looking on whose sons lay dead on Southern battlefields, and sisters whose brothers filled nameless graves in the dark forests of the south."

"'My boy fell defending that flag,'" said an old man as the banner of a certain regiment passed by. The crowd gave way till the color-bearer could let the aged father touch the banner.

The quiet was emphasized by an occasional remnant of an army band playing the same music "to which the men kept step at Shiloh and Missionary Ridge," epochal battles that engulfed many thousands of Iowa troops. All the feeling expressed that day may seem mawkish and sentimental in this modern age. But the reverence then was obvious and profound.

Some notable Iowans carried banners and flags up Capitol Hill to the Statehouse. Voltaire Twombly, winner of the Congressional Medal of Honor, bore the colors of the 2nd Iowa Infantry Regiment. Twombly had carried the regimental banner in the 2nd's famous 1862 charge up the hill in the battle of Fort Donelson in Tennessee.

Twombly was the sixth soldier to carry the banner that day. The previous five had been shot down. Twombly also was knocked off his feet by a partly spent bullet but he got up, grabbed the pole again and leaped the enemy parapet with his comrades to final victory. The 2nd lost 40 men killed and 160 wounded in that charge, a casualty rate of more than 20 percent.

Twombly subsequently was severely wounded at the battle of Corinth and at Jonesboro. A resident of Van Buren County, he was elected Iowa State Treasurer three times after the war.

J.A. Easterly of Britt, Iowa, held high the flag of the 13th Iowa in the parade. Easterly was wounded seven times in the battle of Atlanta. Civil War General J.A. Williamson of Des Moines appeared in the parade astride a white horse and wearing a white vest and long-tailed coat.

Des Moines streets were lavishly decorated with flags and bunting. Large numbers of Chinese lanterns gave the Statehouse the appearance of a fairyland.

"Now the flags are in the golden-domed Capitol," said a final report. "There they will remain forever, where patriots can look upon them for ages to come. It is a fit place in this noble building, this just pride of a great state, to put these honored and priceless treasures."

The report recalled a statement by Samuel Kirkwood, Iowa's Civil War governor, who said: "The heroism of our soldiers has made it a proud privilege to be a citizen of Iowa."

The Worst Epidemic

T he secretary of the Iowa Board of Health ordered cancellation of all public gatherings throughout the state.

"When I say everything, I mean everything," declared Dr. Guilford Summer. "That means no public funerals, no public meetings, no visiting. No travel unless absolutely necessary."

The reason: The deadly 1918 influenza epidemic that was sweeping Iowa, the nation and the world.

More than 42,000 Iowans were quarantined with the flu that October. Estimates placed the real number infected, including unreported cases, at nearer 100,000.

At least 6,500 Iowans died of the highly contagious disease. The toll was nearly 3,000 greater than the 3,540 Iowans who were killed or otherwise died in military service during World War I, which was going on at the same time.

An astounding 10,000 cases showed up among troops training for the war at Camp Dodge northwest of Des Moines. Seven hundred and two soldiers died in the 33 days between September 29 and November 1. That was an average of more than 21 a day and equalled nearly 20 percent of the state's military deaths in that entire war.

"It [the disease] spread through the camp with the speed of a grassfire on a windy day," said an army doctor. "One could not run away from it. It was everywhere."

The flu was believed brought to the camp by a contingent of soldiers from Chicago. There were 35,000 troops training in Dodge at the time.

The camp hospital had a capacity of 2,200 patients. All of a sudden 6,000 very sick soldiers needed care and treatment. The hospital had to spill over into 40 nearby barracks. A force of 100 medical officers, 370 nurses and 1,000 other personnel struggled to meet the crisis. Said a doctor: "Beds vacated by death were taken out to be sterilized; their replacements promptly filled [them], sometimes more than once a day; the problem seemed to be to get the patient into the hospital before he died."

The same physician recalled later: "One of my visions was of the great stack of plain pine coffins that appeared at the morgue every morning, to be filled and hauled away during the night."

Emergency steps were taken throughout the hospital section:

> All civilians were ordered out; face-masked guards patrolled the isolation areas; only emergency operations were performed; no gatherings were permitted; all possible beds were emptied; hospital personnel and patients were masked, but nothing stopped the spread of the disease, and no treatment benefitted the victims.

Nurse Irene Robb wrote to her Des Moines parents:

> Day before yesterday I had five patients die on my ward; three yesterday and one today, and I still have 10 or 12 who may not get well.
>
> I am so tired, and have reached the point where I think sometimes I could throw up my arms and scream, or just drop

down no matter where I am.

    I am not sick at all, nor haven't even a cold, but there is a terrible strain all the time of just being so short of help, and patients dying by the dozens all the time, and having to send for their people, and patients die before they get here, then we have to tell them that the patient died several hours ago.

She told how sick men were brought in on litters so fast "I couldn't get the charts numbered fast enough and beds made up quick enough. The patients on litters were lined up five and six in a row along the outside corridor, waiting their turn to get in. Many of those have died now."

    Eighteen kitchens operated around the clock supplying the huge volume of needed soft-diet meals.

    The authorities issued a warning memo saying: "The virus is contained in discharges from the nose and mouth and is given off in the acts of sneezing, coughing and speaking. The hands, and

RED CROSS NURSES at Camp Dodge, near Des Moines

whatever else, may become contaminated by the discharges, can carry the virus and produce new cases."

Omar Bradley, one of the great American generals of World War II (1941-1945), was a 24-year-old major in 1918 at Camp Dodge. He said of the epidemic: "Those men who had just joined us from Alaska were particularly susceptible. One of the companies which had only 86 men developed 85 cases of influenza, and 25 deaths. Many of my close friends were lost."

The camp command imposed a strict quarantine that prohibited soldiers from leaving the camp except on "special and important missions" and barring all except essential civilians.

Evidently there were numerous places of relaxation in the Camp Dodge neighborhood in those days (which is not surprising in light of a camp enrollment of as many as 35,000 to 50,000 soldiers at a time). A report said "all moving picture theaters and other places of amusement and post exchanges, in or near the camp, were closed. The order also discontinued lectures, religious services and other meetings."

Doctors likewise placed under quarantine the big army base hospital at Fort Des Moines on the other side of the city. More than 1,000 patients were being cared for there, including many wounded in action in Europe.

The crackdowns were disastrous to Des Moines businesses catering to soldiers. The number who "came to town" daily to whoop it up had been tremendous. An inter-urban line ran trains every 30 minutes both ways between the camp and Des Moines on weekends and provided hourly service during the week.

All of a sudden, few uniforms were seen on the street. Theaters, restaurants, dance halls, so-called "temp" bars, taxicabs all suffered.

Movies reported attendance down one-third. Charlie Karras, owner of the Locust Chop House at 115 Locust, said: "My revenue will show a shortage of $50 to $75 for today" (like several hundred dollars in the 1990s). The Kirkwood shooting gallery at 315 Locust reported a "decrease of 75 percent."

Things got much worse later in the month as the numbers of cases piled up. Under the state Board of Health order, all schools, churches, theaters, dance halls and other places of amusement were shut down. (Some dance halls operated five and six nights a week in those days.)

Des Moines police dispersed gatherings, "even in stores and on street corners." Conductors held down the number of passengers riding each streetcar to prevent crowding. Civilians were urged to wear gauze face masks, especially if they worked in restaurants, and so were barbers. The Red Cross received a request for 20,000 such masks for use in hospitals, infirmaries and offices. Whether those masks were ever delivered isn't known.

The flu scourge hit small and large communities alike. Blairstown, a town of 600 in Benton County, reported 100 cases and no doctor available. Two hundred prisoners were ill in Anamosa Reformatory, where the doctor also was sick in bed. The caseload ballooned from 1,000 to 1,500 in four days in Sioux City. Des Moines experienced an increase of 1,000 in one week.

Thankfully the disease faded out about as fast as it had developed. Quarantines were lifted, to the relief of everybody. Modern health authorities do not quarantine flu cases.

The flu was believed responsible for 20 million deaths around the world in 1918. The epidemic has been called the worst visitation of disease on mankind in modern times.

40,000 Witnesses

T hree black soldiers crying prayers were hanged at Des Moines' doorstep.

The executions were carried out July 5, 1918, before 40,000 shaken troops at Camp Dodge northwest of Des Moines.

A court martial found all three guilty of raping a 17-year-old white girl after beating up her Des Moines-soldier date. The attack was said to have taken place outside the Hyperion Golf Club adjoining Camp Dodge.

Woodrow Wilson, president of the United States, reviewed the trial and the sentence and approved both.

The executed men were Rob Johnson, Fred Allen and Stanley Tremble, all of Alabama. A fourth defendant, Will Heard, was acquitted.

It was the only military hanging ever in Iowa and is an unhappy episode in the state's history.

Tens of thousands of men trained at Camp Dodge in 1917 and 1918 for combat service overseas in World War I.

The execution scene that July summer morning was one of awesome proportions. The entire 88th Division was drawn up in a huge hollow square with the gallows in the middle. Every man in the seried ranks carried a rifle. Many of the men in the ranks hadn't slept the night before, knowing what they would be required to witness the next day.

The prisoners marched their final quarter mile, each accompanied by an armed guard. The cries of the condemned men along the way were echoed and re-echoed among the thousands of onlookers. Several fainted and had to be carried away. One deranged soldier broke ranks and ran straight for the gallows but was intercepted.

After the traps had been sprung, one of the men was found to still be clutching a hymnal in death.

Glory?

Young soldiers came "home" from overseas by the dozens almost daily. But there were no colorful parades, no waving flags, no martial music to greet them.

Only army ambulances waited to take them from the railroad station to Fort Des Moines Army Post. Some were able to get off the train by themselves. Others had to be helped because they were minus legs or arms, perhaps both.

Still others were carried off on stretchers.

The men were wounded and sick of World War I of 1917-1918. They were brought by ship and rail from the battlefields of France to the 1,500-bed base hospital the army had built at the army post, a hospital that was done away with after the war's end.

More than 7,500 wounded and ailing were brought to Des Moines in the 1918-1919 period.

Ironically the hospital experienced its toughest day with only one week of the war remaining. Two hundred banged-up and ailing men arrived November 4, 1918. The shooting ended November 11.

Private Ray Chitwood was among the most wounded to reach

Fort Des Moines. Chitwood, 5 feet 5 inches tall, was hit in five places by German fire, probably shrapnel, in the famed Battle of Chateau Thierry in France. One piece of metal went through his right foot, a second hit his right leg, a third lodged in his right chest, a fourth knocked two fingers off his left hand and a fifth struck his mouth and knocked out most of his teeth.

That should have been enough warfare for Chitwood of the 128th Field Artillery, 32nd Division. But no. After stays in overseas hospitals and mending at Fort Des Moines, he was returned to active duty in October 1918. He didn't seem to mind. All he said was: "I guess I'll get there in time to join the boys in Berlin."

But he probably didn't get back overseas at all. Peace was declared the next month. Where his home was is not now known.

At least two later Des Moines notables underwent care and treatment at Fort Des Moines. Colonel E.R. Bennett was wounded while serving with the 168th Infantry in the Rainbow division in France. He was Polk County treasurer in the 1920s.

2nd Lieutenant J.B. Morris suffered shrapnel wounds in his right leg in the brutal Argonne Forest battle in France. He was a patient at the Fort hospital for more than two months in 1919 for treatment of his wounds and arthritis.

Morris was one of 639 blacks to receive army commissions in the black officer training school at Fort Des Moines in 1917. It was the army's first black officer training school ever.

Morris practiced law in Des Moines after the war and long published the *Des Moines Bystander,* a black local newspaper. He lived to be 87 years of age.

As hospitals go, the death rate at the Fort hospital seems to have been low. Fewer than 100 of the surgical, medical and psychiatric patients died. But thousands were discharged with their bodies bearing permanent marks of the blight of war.

The hospital received 543 soldiers with amputations; 392 lost arms in action, 151 lost legs. There were 13 double amputees. A thread of grimness runs through the hospital reports on the amputees:

> Some stumps shrink very rapidly and soon reach a stage suitable for a permanent [artificial] limb fitting, which is not like fitting a pair of shoes. Nature never planned that a human

being should carry his weight on a wooden leg or work with a mechanical arm.

The skill acquired in the use of artificial limbs depends largely on the perseverance and will power of the patient. To aid in this training, we have organized at this hospital walking classes and classes for stump drill.

A civilian wearing two artificial limbs also has been employed to give men points in walking.

The report said that 60 percent of such patients arrived from overseas with unhealed stumps, which was desirable because of the need to take time before fitting each with a permanent artificial limb. One big worry was the possibility that dreaded gangrene or other severe infections would develop. Medicine and medications were almost primitive then compared with at present, as were artificial-limb appliances.

Hospital authorities proudly reported that Captain Charles H. Baldwin had developed an effective limb socket made of ordinary building paper and dextrin glue.

Also treated at the Fort were "foot injuries by the score, hand injuries by the dozen, deformities following nerve injuries, joint injuries, diseased backs, fractured necks, fractured spines, old fractures of necks and arms, muscle and tendon injuries, tuberculosis of joints, osteomyelitis, toe drop, foot drop, contractures and many other injuries incident to the wounds of war."

Iowa Ejected

IOWA U. OUSTED BY 'BIG TEN'

That *Des Moines Register* headline May 26, 1929, hit the state like a thunderbolt.

Big Ten faculty representatives meeting in Chicago voted the drastic action "for the violation of rules prohibiting subsidizing of athletes."

Another basis for the ouster was a belief that the Iowa faculty was losing control of university athletics. That conclusion was based on a recent substantial increase in the power of alumni in operation of the athletic program and the forced resignation of Athletic Director Paul E. Belting.

The ouster took effect January 1, 1930. The action forced the severing of athletic relations with all other Big Ten schools and the cancellation of scheduled games in all sports.

In actual fact, Iowa was out of the conference only one month, from January 1 to February 1, 1930. The university capitulated to conference demands and was reinstated, but the suspension had a devastating effect on Iowa athletics that was felt for years to come.

The immediate casualties included 14 athletes who were declared ineligible, including 1930 football captain Mike Farrah, sensational halfback Oran "Nanny" Pape and four regulars on Coach Rollie Williams's basketball team who were lost in midseason. Football Coach Burt Ingwersen was left with only three letter winners for his 1930 team and with but one conference opponent, Purdue.

Another less spectacular flareup took place in 1958 over the fact that some big name football players often skipped classes in which they were enrolled. They escaped failing grades of "F" by canceling their registrations as soon as football season ended.

And in the late 1980s two sports agents, Norby Walters and Lloyd Bloom, were convicted on charges of extortion, fraud and racketeering. They were accused of bribing two Iowa players to sign professional football contracts while still competing at the university level. Running back Ronnie Harmon received $54,000 and back Devon Mitchell $3,400. Both also succeeded in staying eligible at Iowa by taking patsy courses with little relationship to academics.

In the 1929 blowup, Iowa wasn't the only Big Ten institution under scrutiny for athletic practices. One official said other conference members "have violated conference rules and regulations, but such evidence seems conclusive against Iowa." Other schools named were Wisconsin, Northwestern, Indiana and Ohio. Another report said Chicago was the only school completely clean. (Chicago dropped out of the Big Ten shortly afterward.)

Anger welled up all over Iowa over the university ouster. W.C. Stutslager of Lisbon, member of what is now the state Board of Regents, said: "It is absolutely incredible. I feel that such action is entirely unwarranted." Some 250 incensed students were said in one report to have been talked out of attacking the home of former Athletic Director Belting, who was widely blamed for the Big Ten action. Belting, however, said the students did throw eggs and bricks at his house and he had to call the police.

In an editorial headed "Calling the Kettle Black," the *Register* said: "The fact is, none of the Big Ten schools dare face the issue of amateur and professional squarely and mark a broad line between them that will be religiously observed."

The second-day *Register* headline in the 1929 shocker said: 'SLUSH FUND' IN S.U.I. OUSTER.

By 1993 standards, the fund doesn't seem to have been very slushy. The total distributed to athletes through Iowa City businessmen seems to have been in the range of $5,000 to $10,000 a year, seemingly not all that much for a program. It must be remembered, however, that inflation in the last 60 years has cut the value of the $1 today to perhaps one-tenth what it was then, that $10,000 in 1929 was like $100,000 in purchasing power now. Those were the days when you could go into a restaurant and get a piece of pie and a cup of coffee for 15 cents total. And a loaf of bread and a bottle of milk likewise cost 15 cents total.

What figures did come out didn't indicate very high athletic compensation for the most part, and the money the athletes got was supposed to be pay for jobs they held which were financed by Iowa City businessmen. The athletes were said to have been paid whether they worked or not.

Mayes McClain, a fullback, received $60 a month for a "real estate census" of Iowa City. That job was regarded as a joke by some.

Oran Pape, who was married, also got $60 a month. Where he proved to be an embarrassment to Iowa was in having played pro football before he enrolled in the university. Minnesota charged Pape with professionalism before the 1929 season. Iowa conducted an investigation and cleared the player. Pape then proceeded to defeat Minnesota with a long run late in the 1929 game, as he also had done in the 1928 game.

Iowa afterwards conceded on Pape's "own admission" that he had played pro ball. Two other players, identified only as Fuhrman and Kelsh, also had played professionally and were declared ineligible. The university, however, tried to get Fuhrman reinstated because he had played under his own name and had not tried to hide his identity under an alias. It isn't known whether the Fuhrman effort was successful, but it probably was not. Pape had played as a pro under an assumed name.

Pape, incidentally, lost his life a few years later while serving as an Iowa highway patrolman. He was shot by a bandit. Though fatally wounded, courageous Pape shot and killed the bandit. He was the first state patrolman to die in the line of duty.

The largest reported Iowa compensation for players apparently went to one Tom Stidham. Big Ten Commissioner John Griffith said an alumnus provided Stidham with transportation to Iowa City, where he was met by a Mr. Goltman of the Iowa Supply Company. The player was taken to a fraternity house where a group of men offered him $75 a month. But he said he expected $100 a month, so it is reported he was paid $100 a month in "checks signed by [a] Mr. Williams." Griffith also said Williams reportedly took care of Stidham's university tuition and fees at the business office. (A sum of $100 a month then was as valuable as $1,000 a month is now.) Nothing else was said concerning Stidham in the 1929 reporting.

It seems piddling now but publicity was given to the fact that a number of players had signed notes for their tuition payments, the average note being $45. (Which gives some idea on how much less tuition was in the 1920s.) Under the tougher conference rules in effect then, a player wasn't supposed to even get his tuition paid. Iowa made the point that non-athletes also were permitted to sign notes for tuition in those days. Reports indicated that at least some of the athlete's notes never were paid.

An embattled figure in the controversy was Belting, the resigned athletic director. Whether Belting deserved to be praised or condemned depended on which side one was on.

Belting said University of Iowa President Walter Jessup forced him to resign because he, Belting, had refused to divert athletic funds to subsidize athletes. Belting issued a statement saying his discharge meant surrender to the power of evil in athletics.

A statement issued by three other prestigious Big Ten athletic directors expressed belief that Belting was not responsible "for the condition that has resulted in the action taken by the conference faculty committee." The other directors were Alonzo Stagg of the University of Chicago, Fielding Yost of Michigan and George

Huff of Illinois.

But there were indications that Belting had had a hand in an athletic fund creation.

Furious alumni accused Belting of treachery. Editor W. Earl Hall of the *Mason City Globe-Gazette* was one of three alumni appointed to the University athletic board prior to the ouster action. In an editorial discussing the "slush fund," Hall declared:

> The fund in question bears the soiled fingerprints of Mr. Belting, the former director, who squealed when he lost his job because of the many stupid things he did. Without the knowledge or consent of anybody, he diverted funds from his department and established the loan fund in an Iowa City bank.

There is no question, however, but that the alumni did succeed in downgrading the office of Iowa athletic director. Edward H. Lauer was appointed to succeed Belting but alumni pressure apparently succeeded in getting Jessup to name track coach George Bresnahan to a new position of Director of Intercollegiate Athletics. Commissioner Griffith took a dim view of that appointment. He said "a small group of alumni" was reported as "having boasted" they were going to get Bresnahan that job, with the result that some in the Big Ten felt "sovereignty resided" in those alumni "rather than the University heads."

Another charge that came to the surface said the University registrar had not "for some years" certified the scholastic eligibility of athletes, "that this matter was taken out of the hands of the registrar by the president of the University to permit greater freedom of certifying athletes for conference competition."

Iowa conceded this was true and said that function was taken over by the athletic board "during the directorship of Howard H. Jones [also the football coach] as a result of personal differences between Jones and H.G. Dorcas, the registrar." But another source said the certification policy was okay because it was done with the approval of the Big Ten faculty committee.

What finally cleared the air and set the stage for restoring Iowa to good standing in the Big Ten were the withdrawal of Bresnahan from the athletic directorship and the move declaring the 14 athletes ineligible. Bresnahan stayed on in his longtime post as track coach.

Westbrook Pegler, then a sportswriter for the *Chicago Tribune,* in effect accused other Big Ten schools of hypocrisy for the action against Iowa.

"To be sure, there had been a jingle of unauthorized small money in the locker rooms of Iowa varsity squads," Pegler wrote, "but what's that jingle in the locker rooms of other varsities in the Big Ten? Could that have been nothing but the boys' keys clinking innocently in their pants pockets?"

Another interesting aside of the 1929-1930 situation involved one Everett Case, coach of the Frankfort, Indiana, high school basketball team. Case attended the 1924 summer session at Iowa City taking academic courses.

Iowa basketball coach Justin Barry helped Case in coaching his Frankfort team in the Indiana high school championship tournament, which was a bit unusual.

Then Case needed certain credits to get his Indiana state teaching certificate renewed for the 1926-1927 school year. He came to Iowa City for a couple of days at the beginning of the 1926 summer session. He registered for certain courses but then didn't come back and attend any classes. Even so, Iowa gave him the credits he needed.

The Iowa Liberal Arts College dean explained when questioned that it was not unusual for a former student in good standing to register for work and not attend classes provided he passed a special examination given with the approval of the dean. It developed that such approval hadn't been given. The instructor said he forgot to get that approval.

In addition Frankfort basketball players Robert Spradling and Doyal Plunkett enrolled at Iowa in 1926. Commissioner Griffith suspected collusion involving Case getting the credits and the athletes enrolling at Iowa. The commissioner announced after an investigation, however, that he found no connection and Iowa was cleared.

Badly damaged as it was, the Iowa football team did fairly well in 1930, winning four and losing four. Purdue beat the Hawks 20-0 but the other losses were close ones, to Oklahoma State, Centenary and Marquette, whereas Iowa did beat Nebraska 12-7, Penn State 13-0 and Detroit 7-3 after an easy victory over Bradley in the season's opener.

Where Iowa took a beating was at the box office. After

reaching a then-record $200,000 in football receipts in 1929, the gate fell to a disastrous $42,000 in 1930.

The 1931 season was Iowa's low point. The team didn't score at all in seven of eight games. The Hawks did defeat George Washington University 7–0 for the season's only victory. Coach Ingwersen resigned. His teams had a Big Ten record of six wins, 18 losses and three ties beginning in 1926. He was succeeded by Ossie Solem, who came from Drake to take the Iowa job.

In the 1958 disclosure, the players known to have dropped all courses at the end of the football season were All-American Alex Karras, Collins (Mike) Hagler, Richard (Sleepy) Klein and Bob Commings, later the Iowa football coach.

University officials expressed concern over the dropouts at the time. They felt a star who didn't attend classes set a bad example for younger players. Also, the players lost a full semester and unnecessary costs had been incurred.

One report at the time said there were cases where a player registered for a course, didn't attend one class afterwards and then canceled the course at the close of the football season.

Both Hagler and Klein admitted they didn't go to zoology classes very often. Asked whether he went at all, Hagler said: "My attendance record was very poor but not that poor." He said he didn't mind zoology lab "but I don't seem to get anything out of the lectures," so he rarely went.

The Hagler situation was such that the Big Ten office in Chicago questioned whether he had taken sufficient hours in the football season to be eligible for competition. Iowa's reply was that Hagler had taken nine hours and that could be considered a full load in the Liberal Arts College. The ordinary student semester load was 15 hours. Evidently Hagler's nine hours included physical education courses. Physical education was a division of Liberal Arts.

The Iowa explanation on Hagler satisfied the Big Ten. In the final analysis, however, he wasn't a student at all while he was playing football because he wasn't going to class much and he dropped all the courses he had signed up for once the season was over.

At the same time, however, the rules said an athlete had to show minimum progress towards his academic degree each year to maintain eligibility. An athlete in liberal arts or commerce had to have completed 28 hours as a sophomore, 51 hours as a junior and 76 hours as a senior to be eligible to play. How the players in question stacked up against those requirements wasn't disclosed.

Klein also admitted that he rarely went to zoology classes. He had one year of competition left in 1958 but he chose instead to sign a professional football contract with the Chicago Bears.

Football coach Forrest Evashevski said it was sometimes forgotten that many gridders were excellent students. He cited Frank Bloomquist, Kennie Ploen, Captain John Gibbons and Randy Duncan, all stars of the late 1950s. The coach also commented that "football is secondary to getting an education," and he said post-season bowl games were "over-done." "I don't see how a boy can take part in all those activities and do justice to his school work," the coach added.

Commings and Karras did enroll in Iowa for the second 1957-1958 semester. Their competition was over and both said they planned to get their degrees in physical education.

Commings had dropped German, social science, literature and education at the end of the 1957 season. One report said 8 or 10 athletes dropped German at the season's end. (A foreign language was required for a degree in physical education.) That report said one topnotch athlete hadn't come to foreign language class at all after enrolling in September.

Commings' determination to get his degree was demonstrated in 1958 by the fact that he was taking 17 hours in the second semester, including Spanish, social sciences, masterpieces of literature and football coaching.

Commings was 25 at the time and an earnest player. "To me it was the emotional strain [of going to school and playing football]," he said. "You are always thinking about what happened the week before and what is going to happen the next week. You lack the power to concentrate. If you try to study, you don't get anything out of it. You are glad when the season is over."

Karras said he didn't cut classes except on Fridays when Iowa had an out-of-town game. He said he was taking 16 hours the previous semester before he canceled out. He took 15 hours the second semester, including anatomy, psychology and social science. He said football "isn't a hardship if you've got brains enough in the first place. But if you are borderline, it can be a hardship."

Registrar Red McCarrel said in 1958 that Iowa's scholastic standards were above average for the Big Ten. He said football and basketball players "are about an average cross section" of the student body as a whole.

In connection with grades and eligibility, basketball coach Frank (Bucky) O'Connor endured an unpleasant experience in the athletic department in the late 1950s. He taught a course in basketball coaching. One student was a football player who almost never came to class. The guy wasn't doing very well in his other studies either.

A football coach turned the heat on Bucky to give the player an "A" to help offset poor grades elsewhere. O'Connor gagged at that request but finally reluctantly gave the player a "C." He didn't deserve even that but the football staff wasn't grateful. Bucky was an unpopular person in certain Iowa City circles for a time.

A Run on a Bank

B anker C. W. Fishbaugh sensed one Saturday that trouble was brewing. He was cashier of the Security Trust and Savings Bank of Shenandoah.

Depositors kept coming in a steady stream to withdraw their money. The year was 1931. The Great Depression had taken over Iowa and the rest of the nation.

There was no federal deposit insurance as yet. When a bank closed, depositors lost at least part of their cash, often most of it. Thus, when rumors started that a bank was in difficulty, people hurried in to get their cash. And plenty of banks were, and had been, in trouble in Iowa.

The Shenandoah bank was sound. But no bank could pay off a sudden huge onslaught of depositors demanding their money. Such a visitation was called a "run" on the bank. No bank could afford to tell a line of anxious depositors that there was nothing for them, that the money was all gone.

All the Shenandoah depositors that Saturday gave good reasons for wanting their funds. "They were lending money to a friend," Fishbaugh wrote in a piece for the Burroughs Clearing House, "or they needed money for an unusual cash transaction.

When we closed at 4 o'clock, we knew something was in the wind but we couldn't put our finger on it."

A friend called to warn that a real "run" could be expected Monday. Worried depositors also phoned to ask how the bank was doing. Fishbaugh realized he'd better get ready. He called his correspondent bank in Omaha and said he needed $50,000 cash right away. (An especially large sum in 1931.)

"They [the Omaha bank] said they'd be happy to send the money down but their time locks [on the vault] were set for 10 o'clock Monday morning," Fishbaugh recalled. "This was a blow. We opened each banking day at 9 o'clock. It meant we would have to be open at least three hours before the cash would arrive. We would have to operate all morning on the cash we had on hand." (Shenandoah is about 75 miles south of Omaha, cars were slower and roads were poorer in those days.)

Monday was chilly and rainy. Crowds gathered in front of the bank at 8 a.m., an hour before opening time.

"We were playing for time," Fishbaugh said. "We knew the 'run' was only minutes away and that our limited supply of cash would melt rapidly in the next few hours. We had to make the cash last until the additional money arrived from Omaha, and hope the sight of it would stop the run."

At 9 o'clock sharp, an employee rolled up the curtain on the window, opened the door, and in surged the crowd. First customers were polite and gave the usual excuses for needing the money. None admitted that he or she was trying to get his funds before the bank folded.

"But the crowd grew, tension increased and all pretense was pushed aside," the cashier said. "All that mattered now was the cash. The crowd grew noisier and more unruly. The gathering outside had increased and there was pushing and shoving to get into the bank."

The rain grew heavier outside, "but it wasn't the rain that made the crowd anxious to get inside. They were afraid the money would be all used up before it came their turn."

Strange things happened. People looked at money that had been withdrawn, as if puzzled over what to do with it. Two withdrew cash from savings and redeposited it in their checking accounts. One man withdrew his money and then put it back in the bank in his wife's name.

"We paid out the money slowly, checking each transaction several times," Fishbaugh said. "We were in no hurry, yet we didn't want to appear to be holding up payments. We watched the clock and when it was pointed at ten we gave a sigh. We had withstood the first hour and by now the vaults in Omaha would be open and our money soon would be on its way. If we could keep going another hour or two, we would have a chance."

The flustered bank got some help at a strategic time. A Shenandoah restaurant operator scraped up all the money he had in his place of business and at home. He even robbed his children's piggy banks.

He brought all the change to the window, slapped it down and said in a loud voice: "Count this and be sure you get it right!" He poured the silver and currency on the counter. It looked like a thousand dollars in change. It was beautiful, and what was more, it would take some time to count.

Employees counted that money slowly and then counted it again.

"As we counted," Fishbaugh said, "he [the restaurant man] carried on a steady conversation about how good his business was and how he would be back the next day with another large deposit. We hoped he was right and there would be another day."

The mayor of Shenandoah came in, got up on a chair and told the crowd the bank was in good condition. He didn't get much attention. A lawyer who did his banking elsewhere slipped a $10 bill to Fishbaugh and asked him to deposit it. The lawyer got up on a chair and shouted: "Don't worry about this bank, I have money in it and I'm not worried." He wasn't fibbing. He did have an account, that $10 bill.

Others made reassuring speeches but couldn't divert the people from their purpose, which was to get their money.

"Our cash was starting to dwindle," the cashier said, "and we were now operating mostly with ones and fives. Another hour at the same rate and we would have been down to just silver.

"Just before noon, a large black car drew up to the curb in front of the bank. A large man jumped out waving a pistol. It looked like a scene from the great train robbery. He put on a great show as he yelled for everybody to stand back. Seeing the pistol, the crowd stood back."

The man grabbed a large traveling bag in each hand from the

car. He carried them as if they were heavy indeed and forced his way through the crowd and into the bank.

"He placed the bags on the back counter and turned them upside down," Fishbaugh said, "A cascade of currency fell out, the contents covered the top of the desk. There seemed to be an endless amount of twenties and tens and the money looked like double the amount we had ordered.

"Never before or since have I thought currency looked so beautiful. To the frightened depositors it must have looked like a dream. To us it looked and seemed like a miracle."

The customers stared at the cash. Those in line continued to withdraw their money. "Then it dawned on the mob there was going to be enough to go around," Fishbaugh said.

The break came when one fellow who had just withdrawn his money paused, then slowly turned back to the teller. He looked over his shoulder at the display of money and said: "Heck, I've got no place to put it. I might just as well leave it here."

The Great 1931 Shenandoah bank "run" was over.

A spectacular one-man "run" on the old First National Bank of Marshalltown enlivened that city in 1872.

Greenleaf Woodbury, a notable pioneer, was president of the First National. He and his allies owned 60 percent of the bank stock. H.E.J. Boardman, early attorney and perhaps the richest man in the area, headed a group that held the other 40 percent.

The two groups didn't like each other at all. The showdown came when Boardman, a heavy depositor, came in one morning and started cashing checks. He presented the first check for $8,000, which was paid, and then another for $5,000, which was paid. The teller asked that Boardman write one check covering all the money he wanted. The lawyer responded by presenting a $20,000 check, which was paid.

Tension grew heavier as Boardman continued writing checks. The bank decided to withhold payment for the time being. Messengers hurried to other banks to get currency. One individual, T.J. Fletcher, went by special train to Grinnell to get more cash. Telegrams were dispatched to other banks to send money, pronto.

When Fletcher returned loaded with cash, the bank sent word to Boardman to come and get his money. The lawyer demanded payment of protest fees on the checks that had been turned down before Fletcher got back.

The quarrel reached the courts and even the U.S. Comptroller of the Currency, who pointedly recommended that Woodbury and his associates buy out the Boardman group. This was done.

Later Boardman and his friends took over a private bank. That bank bought the First National more than 30 years later and assumed its name. The First National went broke, along with well over a thousand other Iowa banks, in the years of the Great Depression.

At least three generations of Boardmans practiced law with great success in Marshall County in the 19th and 20th centuries.

Greenleaf Woodbury built an early flour mill on the Iowa River at Marshalltown. Later he added a distillery, which enraged the liquor-hating Methodists. The Reverend C.G. Truesdell, a Methodist minister, prayed: "Oh, God, if need be, wilt thou seize Greenleaf Woodbury by the hair of his head and hold him over the fires of hell that he may be taught the terrors of an avenging God."

There is no record of God ever having seized Woodbury by the hair, but the distillery disappeared generations ago and is now thoroughly forgotten. So, for that matter, is the flour mill.

Toothless Farmers

Life has become a burden. We are down and out.

I can count my friends by the score who are too shabby to attend a friend's or relative's funeral.

One farmer offered anybody his whole crop of grain if that person would pay his taxes.

Health is being undermined by the lack of care of teeth. There are literally hundreds of toothless farm men and women. Poor health necessitated the pulling of teeth. Heaven only knows when there will be money enough to buy false teeth. First the children must be clothed and fed.

Mrs. Warren Johnson wrote those heartfelt words to the *Des Moines Register* in January 1932, near the bottom of the Great Depression. She was a Hardin County farm wife. Her article appeared under the front page headline "An Iowa Farm Woman Speaks Up."

This was the period when a story from Grinnell told of a

father who dug up the coffin of his little daughter in a cemetery and reburied the child in his garden. Then he sold the cemetery lot for $5 and spent the money on shoes for his two remaining children. (Shoes were much cheaper then than now.)

The Depression didn't hit just little people. Iowa Governor Clyde I. Herring lost his beautiful home at 180 Thirty-seventh Street in Des Moines in 1933. He was unable to make the payments on a $37,000 mortgage held by a bank. The governor and his family stayed in the home, however, and paid the bank $125 a month rent. He got enough money together later to regain legal possession of the property.

Herring had been a millionaire automobile dealer and real estate investor. The economic downturn just about wiped him out.

Here's how the Depression inflicted so much damage in Iowa:

- Farm prices sank to unbelievable levels, corn as low as 8½ cents a bushel, hogs $3 or less per 100 pounds, cattle $1.50 to $5 and $6 per 100 pounds. (Hogs topped $60 in late 1990 and cattle sold above $80 at times.)
- Unemployment soared to 25 percent nationally, with 15 million jobless in a work force of 60 million. A job that paid $25 or $30 a week was something to hang on to, and to protect. As late as 1936 unemployed Iowans and their families totaled nearly 450,000—18 percent of the state's population.
- Debts became unmanageable as prices dropped. There was no way for a farmer to pay his interest, taxes and expenses on land carrying a mortgage of $300 an acre. Iowa's average land values sank from a high of $254 an acre in 1919 to $68 in 1933. (The 1990 average was around $1,200 an acre.)
- One Iowa farmer in every seven lost his land by foreclosure between 1926 and 1931. Creditors took over five million acres belonging to 33,000 farmers in that period.
- Insurance companies, banks and other corporations ultimately found themselves unwilling owners of farmland equivalent to the rural areas of 11 of the state's 99 counties. The lenders didn't want the land. But they had lent the money entrusted to them by policyholders and depositors and they had to protect those investments by foreclosures.

- More than 1,200 Iowa banks went broke and depositors lost many millions of dollars in savings and checking accounts. Congress had not yet authorized federal deposit insurance. Bank stockholders lost their shirts. They not only lost the value of their stock; they had to pay additional assessments equal to the original cost of the stock, which was the law at the time.
- Unlucky bankers emerged as principal villains in the vast tragedy. Iowans chuckled over a parlor story about a banker who got a farmer's daughter pregnant. "Don't worry, I'll marry her," the banker said. "Oh no you won't," retorted the farmer. "I'd rather have a bastard in the family than a banker."
- Some 50,000 Iowa families clogged the relief rolls. One Des Moines family chopped up and burned its furniture to keep warm in winter. Another family burned all its player-piano rolls.

Register columnist Harlan Miller told of seeing thousands of homeless sleeping in Grant Park on Chicago's lakefront in 1931. Miller wrote: "Covered with ragged coats, they slump on couches of grass, leaves, ragged blankets and newspapers. Most of them are sheepish, humble, bewildered, illogically ashamed of a misfortune that was only fractionally their fault."

Miller said 200 women had to sleep in Chicago parks. One woman slept under a porch with her 6-year-old daughter.

Corn is basically a human food, directly or indirectly. But corn was so cheap that some Iowans burned it instead of coal to heat homes and other buildings. In Swaledale, Iowa, both the Methodist church and the poolhall bought corn as a heating fuel for 10 cents a bushel—delivered.

Hamburger sold for as little as 5 cents a pound in some places and skim milk for 10 cents a gallon. The Jack Lazarus Market on Forest Avenue in Des Moines sold boneless rolled beef roast for 15 cents a pound.

Such prices didn't help persons without jobs or money (at least until they managed to get on relief). But those with paychecks still coming in often lived pretty well. And most people did have jobs. One person in four was unemployed but the other three were still working.

On the other hand, consider the plight of August Weger, a McGregor farmer. He shipped five calves to market in Chicago in January 1933. Instead of getting paid for the calves, he received a bill for $1.98. Shipping, feed costs and commissions exceeded the sale price of the calves by $1.98.

Many people think the Depression started with the stock market crash of 1929 and ended about 1934. Actually, it began much earlier—in 1920 for farmers, bankers and others—and continued in some respects up to the outbreak of World War II in 1941.

The most dramatic price break in agriculture took place in 1920 when corn nosedived from $1.75 a bushel to 67 cents a bushel between June and December, a 60 percent drop in six months.

But conditions were the most desperate in the 1929-1934 period.

Mrs. Warren Johnson and her husband started farming in Hardin County in 1908. Thus, she saw the whole agricultural depression develop. In her message in the *Register,* she pointed out how prices continued to sag in 1932.

> Eggs are selling at 8 to 12 cents a dozen. In 1929, at this time of the year, eggs brought 26 cents. In 1930 they were 32 cents and in 1931 an even 18 cents.
>
> A 30 dozen case of eggs, about one week's eggs from the average farm flock, is required to buy a pair of shoes.

She said that when hogs sell for about $3.50 per 100, "no one can pay debts." The price of hogs, she added, was little above what her parents received after the Civil War.

> Overalls and cotton dresses again are the mark of a farmer and they are well patched. A few years ago, the dancehalls were full of farmers trying to drown themselves in the pleasures of the day. Vast crowds flocked to farm picnics and to hear politicians clamor about our plight.
>
> Today, worn out with the struggle, with no money to buy gas or pay the fiddler, these people sit at home, brooding over their plight. It's hard to even crack a joke.
>
> Families were bickering under the strain.
>
> The seriousness of getting food and shelter has so worked on the nerves that husband and wife have become intolerant of each other. Parents and children clash. Adults think youth

careless and extravagant. Youths think adults harsh, stingy
and intolerant.

The Iowa farmers of 50 are largely a homeless, insolvent,
spirit-broken class of men, men who 20 years ago had all the
earmarks of becoming the backbone of the middlewest.

Getting shoes was a particular problem with families, she
went on, "and the high school girl's stockings are a worry forever."

One Iowa mother met the clothing crisis in her family by
making children's garments out of fabrics she cut from seat
cushions and seat backs of abandoned automobiles in a junk yard.

Many moms used flour sacks in making children's clothes.
Brand names of flour showed up in unexpected places. When one
high school girl leaned over, she displayed the words "Mother's
Best" across the seat of her underwear.

Communists in Iowa

M other Bloor stirred up plenty of trouble in northwest
Iowa during the farm violence of the Great
Depression.

Mother Bloor was a rabble-rousing Communist from North
Dakota. Her son Harold Ware was a Communist leader. Lem
Harris was an eastern Communist, or Red, as they were called.

The three were assigned by the American Communist Party
to create all the turmoil they could in the farm belt during the
troubled 1930s.

The Communists sought to unite distressed farmers with the
millions of unemployed in the cities into a major Red force. It
didn't work. But the Communists made their presence felt.

One violent episode involving two *Des Moines Register*
newsmen stemmed in part from Mother Bloor. Farm editor Jim
Russell and photographer Maury Horner drove to Sioux City in
1932 to cover a big rural demonstration.

They found Mother Bloor haranguing a crowd to a fever
pitch in a park. The newsmen were not welcome.

According to Horner:

Jim pulled up the car close so I could get a picture of Mother on a hayrack talking to the big bunch of farmers. When I got up on the front of the car to take the picture, they said: "There they are, the sons of bitches!" The farmers left Mother Bloor standing there and all came after us, hundreds of them.

They surrounded the car. They shoved me into the car and kicked me. They let me keep the camera at the moment. I got a bruise out of a kick.

Then they lined up on the side of the car where Jim was sitting at the wheel. The window was down. They went past and each took a poke at Jim as they went by. He didn't have a chance to get the window up.

Then they pulled me out of the car and took the camera. They busted the camera into pieces. A guy on the running board said: "You sons of bitches get out of here!" At one point they almost tipped over the car. It was on two wheels. And somebody heaved a big rock through the back window. They were vicious.

The crowd stood in front of the car. Jim asked me what he should do. I said, "Run over 'em." The crowd split and let us by.

A blow Jim took on the left side of the head damaged his ear. He wasn't able to hear out of that ear the rest of his life.

Did the Communists play a major role in the numerous instances of violence around northwest Iowa? Iowa Attorney General Edward L. O'Connor believed they did. He said, "We have discovered that a Communist center in Sioux City has been actively engaged in egging on the organization. Many engaged in terrorism in the district are not in financial difficulties. They are mostly of the type that like to make trouble."

The "organization" that O'Connor referred to was the Farmers' Holiday Association. It was the heart of the protest movement and was out in front in clashes around the farm belt.

Many on the picket lines out on the highways and in the mortgage foreclosure struggles belonged to the Holiday Association. But whether all involved in the violence were farmers was a matter of debate.

Major General Park Findley of the Iowa National Guard laid a large part of the blame on the Communists. He made the charge while on martial law duty in Crawford County. And Iowa Governor Clyde L. Herring declared the leaders in the Primghar and Le Mars attacks were not farmers at all. On the other hand, Farmer Morris Cope, a ringleader at both places, declared, "We weren't bad fellows up there. We were good people, good citizens."

Mother Bloor did open an office in Sioux City, the center O'Connor referred to. National Guardsmen raided the place and seized Communist literature. One circular urged a farm march on the Statehouse in Des Moines and also accused President Roosevelt and Governor Herring of being tools of the big bankers.

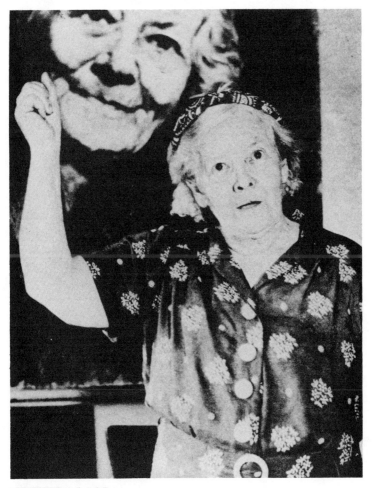

MOTHER BLOOR
Courtesy of the Des Moines Register

Bloor also opened a temporary office in Le Mars and held a number of rural meetings in that area for the purpose of revving up the farmers.

The Holidayers got their name from the idea that all farmers should "take a holiday" and not send any commodities and foodstuffs to market, and not allow anybody else to do so either. But stopping or even slowing down marketing proved to be an impossible task.

Communist Harold Ware tried hard to work with the Holiday group, even attempted to take charge. The demonstrating farmers welcomed Communist help when directed toward achieving higher prices or preventing foreclosures. But few apparently went along with the agitators beyond that.

There was no doubt about the Red qualifications of Ware and Harris. Ware later was a key man in setting up a Communist cell within the U.S. Department of Agriculture in Washington. Harris had come from a wealthy family, had been a Harvard student but was an admitted Red.

What ended the protests, and the slim hopes of the Communists, was President Franklin Roosevelt's New Deal. In late 1933, the federal government began lending farmers 45 cents a bushel on sealed corn, 20 to 22 cents above the market. That put badly needed cash into the farmers' pockets and all but collapsed the Holiday movement.

Two Communist candidates appeared on the 1940 Iowa election ballot. Earl Browder, nationally known Red leader, polled only 1,524 votes for president out of 1.2 million cast in the state. Charles Speck, Denison farmer, got a paltry 1,230 votes for governor. Communists held their Iowa convention in the old downtown Youngerman Building in Des Moines. Forty attended.

Other Communists surfaced from time to time in Iowa during the general period. In 1938 Bill Sentner, St. Louis labor leader and Communist, played a major role in a large-scale Maytag strike in Newton. And one Helen Woods Birnie testified in a 1959 lawsuit that she was sent into Iowa in 1933 to serve as a "Communist agitation propaganda director" and to do labor defense work for the Red cause.

A little Red story that brought smiles nationwide came out of the homestead near Granger in central Iowa in the mid-1930s. Granger priest L.G. Ligutti said one homestead resident had been a Communist.

"But he isn't a Communist any more," the father explained. "He owns two cows now." In other words, he had become a capitalist with property of his own.

A Judge and a Rope

A farm mob dragged a judge off his bench.

The mob took District Judge Charles C. Bradley out in the country near Le Mars in northwest Iowa, roughed him up, and started to hang him.

The attackers demanded Bradley agree to sign no more mortgage foreclosures on farmland. He refused, even though he was in danger of losing his life. He had 15 foreclosure cases pending. He said he hadn't had time to study them.

The mobsters forced the judge to his knees to pray; put handfuls of dirt and a greasy truck hubcap on his head; took down his pants and filled them with mud; threatened him with castration; tightened a rope around his neck. Still the courageous Bradley held fast.

In the end it was the mob that wilted and fled, leaving the judge shaken and alone on a country road. He had a rope burn on his neck, blood on his lips, grease and dirt in his hair and clothes but wasn't injured much.

The vicious treatment of the 53-year-old judge took place April 27, 1933, during the desperation of the Great Depression. The attack was the culmination of widespread violence that began welling up around Iowa and the Midwest the year before, in 1932.

On the day of the Bradley assault, top price paid to farmers for hogs in the nearby Sioux City market was a deeply depressed $3.85 per 100 pounds, less than four cents a pound. The cattle range was a dismal $1.50 to $6 per 100 pounds. Other commodity prices were as dire.

Debt-ridden farmers fought bitterly against their plight. There was no way with such prices that many could pay the principal and interest on their mortgages, let alone taxes and living expenses. They demanded that the courts, mortgage holders, Congress, and the Iowa Legislature all halt mortgage foreclosures.

Mistreating Judge Bradley was but one example of major Iowa violence. The farmers also resorted to hard-hitting tactics sometimes used by labor unions in cities. Thousands of farmers manned picket lines set up along highways to keep trucks from reaching markets with loads of agricultural produce. The idea was to push prices up by reducing supplies of foods available for public consumption (meat, milk, butter, eggs and grain).

The militant national Farmers' Holiday Association issued the call for picketing, saying the farmers should "take a holiday" from sending foodstuffs to market. Association president was Milo Reno of Des Moines, an evangelistic, bull-voiced, longtime head of the Iowa Farmers Union.

Reno declared he opposed violence but he never let up on inflaming the farmers. Pitched battles broke out on the roads between pickets on one side and officers of the law and truckers on the other. Big traffic jams resulted, also beatings, destruction of property, gunfire, wounds and even death.

CHARLES C. BRADLEY
Courtesy of the Des Moines Register

But the flow of foodstuffs to market wasn't slowed down much. There were too many roads to picket, too many markets, too many farmers who wanted to sell their produce despite the "holiday." Nevertheless the hostilities often were spectacular and virulent.

Two things should be noted. First, the activists were but a small minority of Iowa farmers. Then, farmers were by no means the only direct sufferers from the price collapse and the increase in foreclosures. The situation was devastating as well for depositors, who lost millions of dollars when banks had to close because farmers couldn't make payments on their mortgages. Those losers included a lot of "little people" in town as well as the country. (Insurance on bank deposits had not yet arrived.)

The same applied to insurance companies, which lost a lot of policyholders' money when mortgage debts couldn't be collected on farms.

Here's the kind of thing that happened: A lender had to foreclose on the 220-acre Joe Jindrich farm near Walford in Benton County. The mortgage was $100 an acre, or $22,000 total. But the property brought only $47.10 an acre at the foreclosure sale, or $10,362. Thus, the lender fell $11,638 short of recovering the full amount of the original loan.

Similarly, the Burlington Joint Stock Land Bank had to sell the 163-acre Fred Taylor farm near Morning Sun for only $35 an acre, or a total of $5,705. The mortgage, however, was $14,994, or $9,289 more than the amount realized in the sale.

Such defaults helped cause more than 1,200 Iowa banks to fold during the Depression and Iowans to lose a lot of hard-earned money in savings and checking accounts.

Nevertheless, there was a widespread feeling among farmers that banks and insurance companies were greedy monsters, trying to grab all the land they could. G. Foster Holmes, a Cedar Rapids attorney, called that impression "utterly false."

Pointing to the fact that 348 Iowa banks were in receivership in early 1933 alone, Holmes said foreclosures "have always been a last resort. Companies have made every effort to avoid it."

Whatever the ramifications, a major buildup of intimidation and violence developed as the Depression deepened.

A strike by 500 dairy farmers in August of 1932 provoked milk dumping in the Sioux City area. Pickets stopped a truck from Moville and spilled 400 gallons of milk in a ditch. A truck from Cherokee was halted in Kingsley and the interceptors poured 100 gallons of milk in the street. Milk from another truck was dumped into a river. An additional 1,100 gallons was similarly destroyed at Council Bluffs.

What the dairy farmers wanted was more money for their milk. They were getting $1 per 100 pounds at Sioux City. That's two cents a quart. They demanded $2.17 per hundred or more than four cents a quart. (These were the times when a shopper could buy a quart of regular milk for five cents in a store and skim milk sometimes sold for as little as 10 cents a gallon.)

The Sioux City strikers finally settled for $1.80 a 100 or 3.6 cents a quart. Predictions were heard that meant families would have to start paying at least eight cents a quart for milk in Sioux City, which mothers didn't like at all!

Another dairy conflict developed one cold winter night when pickets stopped a southbound truck carrying 1,000 one-pound prints of butter to Sioux City. The truck was halted at the Highway 75 bridge over the Floyd River at James, Iowa. The driver tried to argue. That irritated the pickets, who dumped the butter over the bridge railing. They picked up the truck, turned it around and sent the driver back north.

VIOLENCE at a milk blockade
Courtesy of the Des Moines Register

The pickets had second thoughts about wasting all that butter. Several went down to the river and retrieved a lot of it off the river ice. The butter was loaded onto a truck. One John Sokolovske and another picket drove down the road and put from two to five pounds of butter in each farmer's mailbox between James and Kingsley, Iowa.

Butter played a bizarre role in a dangerous caper. Pickets smeared butter all over a section of concrete to make driving hazardous for truckers. Plymouth County Sheriff Ralph Rippey came along and skidded off the slippery road and into a ditch. He was uninjured.

Rippey and his deputies escorted a number of caravans of livestock trucks traveling the picketed highways. Sometimes the trucks got safely through despite pickets and obstacles. Another time a caravan was halted and Rippey decided not to try to ram the vehicles through. Which was just as well as it turned out. Pickets had planted dynamite in a culvert ahead. They intended to touch off an explosion when the trucks reached that point. Loss of life would have been likely.

Sometimes pickets were arrested for interfering with the flow of traffic. Forty-three were jailed at Council Bluffs. A thousand farmers threatened to smash into the jail and free the prisoners. Declared Sheriff P.A. Lainson, "I don't want any bloodshed and you boys don't either. But I've got to meet my maker sometime, and it might as well be tonight as any other time."

An outright battle was averted when Council Bluffs authorities agreed to release the prisoners on bonds of $100 each.

On the other side of the state, a "howling mob" of 500 besieged the jail at Clinton. They demanded release of three men in custody for illegal picketing. But cooler heads prevailed and there was no frontal attack.

An angry crowd was more successful at making a farce out of a barnyard sale in southern Iowa. The sale was held on the H.A. Gilliland farm west of Lamoni. The farmer had gone broke and so had the Lamoni State Savings Bank which financed him. The bank held a chattel mortgage on his assets such as farm animals and equipment.

The bank receiver scheduled an auction. A big crowd of hostile farmers arrived. The auctioneer wanted to postpone the sale. The crowd wouldn't let him. The crowd would permit only unbelievably low bids. A team of horses worth $200 sold for $4, a wagon for 25 cents, cows for $1 each and brood sows for 75 cents each. The entire sale brought in only $35. A number of like auctions occurred elsewhere in Iowa. In such cases the successful bidders returned the assets to the bankrupt farmer.

Many times a county auctioned off farmland for nonpayment of taxes. More than 600 antagonistic farmers jammed a delinquent tax sale in Winnebago County. There was no sale. Nobody dared bid.

On January 4, 1933, more than three months prior to the seizure of Judge Bradley, violence erupted outside the courthouse at Le Mars. Some 400 farmers gathered that winter day around the courthouse steps where Plymouth County Sheriff Rippey held a sale of the foreclosed John A. Johnson farm.

A call for bids brought a sealed proposal to buy the property for $30,000. That was the amount of the original mortgage. Attorney Herbert S. Martin submitted the bid in behalf of the New York Life Insurance Company, the mortgage holder.

Total debt against the Johnson farm, however, had risen to $33,000 because of unpaid interest and taxes. Thus, had the $30,000 offer been accepted, the owner would have been left facing an additional debt of $3,000 plus losing his farm.

Announcement of the $30,000 bid was the signal for action. Farmers knocked Attorney Martin off his feet and dragged him down the steps. Sheriff Rippey was pushed aside. The farmers slapped Martin and threatened him with a coat of tar and feathers. They brandished a rope in the lawyer's face and told him he might be hanged unless he boosted the bid to $33,000. He said he could not without company approval.

"Get it then!" the crowd shouted.

Martin hurriedly wrote a telegram to the company asking permission to raise the bid. He ended the message with these words: "Rush answer. My neck at risk."

Back in a few hours came company approval. That crisis was over.

The extra $3,000 debt in the John A. Johnson case was known as a deficiency judgment, a very sore point with foreclosed farmers all over Iowa. They thought it totally unfair to be stuck with that additional debt on top of loss of their farms. But the lenders couldn't be blamed either. They were left with having to pay the

MORRIS COPE
Courtesy of the Des Moines Register

delinquent property taxes. And federal law required that they pay income taxes on the uncollected interest as well, something they could ill afford.

Elimination of the additional judgment enabled the John Johnsons to stay on the farm another year under a state redemption law.

Meanwhile, the capitulation of Attorney Martin on the outside steps didn't satisfy the protesters. Some 30 farmers jammed their way into the office of District Judge Chan Pitts in the courthouse. They demanded that he stop signing foreclosures. Judge Pitts said: "I sympathize deeply with the farmers in northwest Iowa. They have been flooded out. Drought and depression have cut their crops and incomes. But the law says I must sign foreclosure decrees when called upon to do so." He also said that what the farmers demanded was "against my oath of office."

"With conditions like they are, I would think you would be more worried about your neck than your oath of office," said Morris Cope, 27, a Farmers' Holiday Association leader. Cope farmed near Kingsley, Iowa.

Judge Pitts quieted the protesters in this way: He agreed to write to Governor-elect Clyde L. Herring in Des Moines recommending emergency state action to delay at least some foreclosures. The judge suggested passing a new law forbidding foreclosures for a period of five to seven months in cases where the farmer was left facing an additional deficiency judgment debt. The rebelling farmers departed.

After he was inaugurated governor of Iowa early in January of 1933, Herring issued a proclamation calling on all mortgage holders and other creditors to refrain from foreclosures until the new legislature had had time to act. Most observers believed Herring did not have the authority under the law to issue such a proclamation. It did not seem to have had much effect anyway.

The *Des Moines Register* feared the violence might scare investors from ever again lending money on Iowa land. Said the *Register:* "Without loan value, land will have no sale value."

Out on the rural battlefront, the warfare took on a grimmer tone with the appearance of guns. Nobody was injured in one early episode. The Van Buren County sheriff seized a farmer armed with a shotgun. The sheriff served a legal paper on the farmer in connection with a foreclosure. Said the sheriff, "When I grabbed him, [he] called to his wife and she ran in the house and came out pointing a rifle at us. We left."

More serious was an incident at night on a highway near Cherokee. Fourteen pickets were wounded by pellets from shotgun blasts fired from two speeding cars. The shooters were not apprehended. The wounds were painful but not serious.

Much worse was a gun battle February 3, 1933, west of Sioux City in South Dakota. R.D. Markell, 67, of Union County, South Dakota, was headed for Sioux City in a truck carrying 1,000 gallons of milk. With him were three sons. Two miles west of town they came upon a telephone pole and a spiked plank blocking the highway. An armed force of 75 pickets waited in the ditches.

Markell got out of the truck and rolled the pole off the road. Somebody fired. That touched off a volley of shots from both sides. Markell was hit seven times in the abdomen. Though seriously wounded, he removed the spiked plank too. One son suffered a wound in the head and had a thumb shot also. Another son was shot in the head.

Blood streaming from their faces, the two young Markells stood among milk cans and returned the fire. Picket Nile Cochran of Moville was shot in the neck and head. Another picket lost a thumb.

When it was all over, the truck was riddled with bullets. Both front tires were punctured and the windshield and door glass shattered. The elder Markell died. His sons and the pickets recovered.

Picket Cochran was arrested and convicted of manslaughter in a trial in South Dakota. He was given a three-year penitentiary sentence.

Cochran said the pickets "didn't mean to harm anyone and were only trying to protect our own interests."

"We brought along our guns only to frighten the Markells," he added, "and we didn't think there would be any shooting. The pickets figured that if enough of them were seen on the highway with firearms, the Markells would not attempt to run their truckload of milk through. We were mistaken, however."

Cochran added, "I don't mind so much going to jail this time. I just got through butchering a cow and two hogs so my wife and children are provided for."

Other pickets said they objected to the Markell milk being brought in from outside the "Sioux City milk shed" and moving into a restricted marketing territory.

On the following March 13 about 3,000 members of the Farmers' Holiday Association staged a march on the Legislature in Des Moines. The legislators had passed a law permitting the courts to delay foreclosures for two years, or until March 1, 1935. But the angry farmers weren't satisfied. They demanded an outright delay of two years "without expensive receiverships" on all foreclosures. They wanted to be able to ignore a foreclosure suit without penalty for two years.

The seething farmers swarmed into the Statehouse and completely disrupted both the House and Senate in session.

"You didn't know what was going to happen that day," recalled State Representative Dewey Goode, a Bloomfield Republican. "They [the farmers] were actually carrying pitchforks and ropes in some instances. But I don't think they had any intention of using them."

State Senator Leo Elthon, Fertile, Iowa, Republican, said, "They were angry. They were losing their farms and they barged right down to the desks in the Senate and started criticizing the senators. They called me all sorts of names."

State Representative Art Hanson, Inwood Republican, found a "big fat lady" sitting on top of his desk. She stayed there during the entire invasion.

"There was a real fear of violence," Hanson said. "It was a serious situation. You can never tell what might happen when the mob spirit takes hold of normally sensible people."

The farmers finally went away peaceably but never did get exactly what they wanted from the legislators.

The violence continued. On April 18 and 19, farmers prevented Sheriff Rippey from ousting Ed Durband from a foreclosed farm near Le Mars. When the crowd hesitated, Morris Cope shouted, "Didn't you fellows come here to stop this? Then why the hell don't you do it? Grab that sheriff!"

The crowd seized Rippey, took the shells out of his gun, searched his briefcase, poured water into the fuel tank of his car. He departed but not in his immobilized car.

Cope again was a ringleader on April 27, the day of Gethsemane for Judge Charles Bradley. The violence on that day, however, started not at Le Mars but in the O'Brien County courthouse at Primghar, 44 miles away. Land belonging to one John Shaffer was scheduled to be sold at a sheriff's sale at Primghar.

County telephones buzzed the night before as Holiday Association members laid plans to converge on Primghar at dawn, ready to do battle. They came from all directions in the early morning darkness, many from Plymouth County.

O'Brien Sheriff Ed Leemkuil got wind of the coming onslaught. He mobilized 22 deputies in the courthouse, all armed with sawed-off pool cues. The sale was scheduled for the balcony upstairs.

The farmers crowded into the courthouse. Barring the way up the stairs were the waiting deputies, three on each step.

A man came down and said, "Everybody out fellows. We've made a settlement." Cope yelled, "Everybody stop where you are! There's something wrong here!"

Suddenly there was a shout, "They're selling the man's farm from the balcony!"

The farmers charged the deputies, who swung their clubs with abandon. A report said eight or 10 farmers were injured, most slightly. Cope, however, suffered a "battered head." He later described his injury this way, "A deputy hit me over the head and fractured my skull. I bled out of my nose and ears. They carried me to a doctor's office. I had to have an x-ray in Hartley, Iowa."

The deputies held fast until the farm was sold for $7,400 on a bid offered by O.H. Montzheimer, attorney for an insurance company. The rioting evidently had its effect, however, even though the farmers had been repulsed. An arrangement was reached under which Shaffer was given the opportunity to buy back the farm near Calumet, Iowa, for $6,500, or $900 less than the foreclosure minimum.

The farmers inflicted a bit of strange retribution on Attorney Montzheimer. They demanded that he come out of the courthouse, get down on his knees and kiss an American flag.

"I'll do it if it will stop this riot," he said, and he did. Several of the deputies kissed the flag as well.

A doctor meanwhile told Cope to "go home and put an ice pack on your head because if it gets to bleeding on your brain, that's serious." Above all, the doctor said, "don't get excited."

Never was a doctor's order more thoroughly disobeyed. Cope said he had "a splitting headache" but he returned to the Primghar courthouse and resumed what undoubtedly was the wildest day of his life. His head was swathed in a white bandage. That caused him to stand out in a crowd, which proved to be a great disadvantage in the activities that followed.

Judge Charles Bradley had previously presided at the Primghar proceeding which resulted in foreclosure of the mortgage against the Shaffer farm. Cope thought that Judge Bradley was at Primghar that day. Cope found out that Judge Pitts was there, not Bradley, who was holding court at Le Mars.

Cope got out on the Primghar balcony and told the crowd, "Now what we should do, instead of going around fighting deputies, getting our skulls fractured, we should go in a body down to Le Mars. We should ask Judge Bradley to give us the benefit of the doubt."

Cope said later, "All I had to do was suggest it and everybody went to Le Mars."

More than 300 farmers mobilized in the Le Mars baseball park about 4:30 that afternoon, Cope among them. He said, "Let's go up and throw the fear of God into Bradley." That was the signal to converge on the courthouse.

Bradley was a slender, average-sized man, a bachelor, clean shaven, with glasses and a wan smile. He took his judicial responsibilities seriously. He was not the kind of person to be pressured into anything.

The judge was in his office when the farmers entered the courtroom. He quickly took his place on the bench. The room soon filled, with many farmers standing along the walls when Cope walked in.

"They clapped and whistled and everybody gave me a big hand," Cope said. "The judge rapped the gavel to beat the band. Rap rap rap. Order in the court or I'll clear the courtroom."

The judge asked what the visit was all about. Cope said the farmers were looking for justice, that they had been to the Legislature in Des Moines and had gotten no results. At that point the judge commanded, "No smoking."

Cope acknowledged that several farmers were smoking cheap cigars and "a few had pipes."

Fred [Mox] Blankenburg, one of the farmers, came in and walked down the aisle, looking for a seat.

"Blankenburg had a little old cap on," Cope continued, "and the judge hollered, hats off in my courtroom!"

"That was what really brought the battle on," commented one farmer. "He said it was his courtroom. It wasn't his courtroom any more than mine. I'm a taxpayer."

The judge's orders against smoking and cap-wearing had been greeted with "jeers and shouts of 'take him out!' and 'let's get him!'"

What caused the final blowup never was entirely clear. One person in the crowd reported Bradley said, "I don't have to listen to you farmers." The same person said a voice in the crowd responded, "The hell you don't!"

The crowd rushed the bench.

"They were piling on him right away," Cope said. "They surrounded him. Somebody was clipping him on one side. Then somebody would nick him on the other side. Somebody hollered 'take him out!' and out they went."

Cope said that when he got out into the crowded hall "some big tall skinny guy had the judge on his hip, with feet and hands dangling."

"The guy reached down and grabbed the judge by the seat of his pants," Cope added. "The guy swung the judge up over his head. I thought maybe he was going to drop the judge over the rail onto the floor below. Instead the guy threw the judge on top of the crowd. They pushed and tumbled the judge down the stairs. That didn't do him any good."

Outside in the courthouse yard shouting farmers again demanded that Bradley sign no more foreclosures. He declined to make such a pledge and was "jerked around and slapped."

Martin Rosburg of Hinton said he told Bradley at this point, "Now judge, this is too bad. This is a mistake. The thing to do is go back upstairs and talk this thing over. We're in trouble and we just want to talk this thing over with you. We want you to give us a little consideration." The judge didn't reply.

Somebody in the crowd said, "Only one thing to do with a guy like this is to hang him." Another voice asked, "In the courthouse yard or out in the country?" The reply, "Just as well take him out in the country. There are machine guns in the sheriff's office."

Sheriff Rippey was nowhere in sight, nor any other officers to challenge the mob.

Unhindered, the farmers loaded the judge into a truck belonging to Bock Brothers of Hinton. Six or eight rioters got on the truck.

"We didn't know what to do with the judge," Rosburg said afterwards, "so we decided to give him a little hair tonic. There was a half-pint of whisky under the front seat. We said to the judge, 'Here's where you are going to have a drink on us guys.' Bradley said nothing and clenched his teeth when the bottle was offered." Rosburg picked up a screwdriver.

"I pried his mouth open, you're damn right," Rosburg related. Rosburg poured liquor down the unwilling judge's throat.

"The way it turned out, that was the best damn thing I ever did in my life," Rosburg said. "That guy had been in the hospital right before and the whisky gave him a little stimulant."

Rosburg may have been right about the dose of whisky. News stories from the 1933 period said Bradley suffered from heart disease, had been in poor health for some time and had suffered a serious illness in the preceding month. Had the judge died of a heart attack in the middle of the assault, some of the rioters might have been convicted and hanged. (Iowa had capital punishment at the time.)

The judge's assailants took him a mile and a half east of Le Mars. He staggered and fell as he alighted from the truck. One man pushed him over two different times.

Somebody put a blindfold on the judge. There was talk of whether to hang him or drag him tied to a rope behind a moving car.

He was pulled to his feet and a rope was placed around his neck and thrown over an electric sign on a pole nearby. Several times he was given a last chance to agree to do what the mob demanded about foreclosures. He refused.

Bradley later testified:

> I told the men I had to act according to the law and uphold my oath of office. They then put the rope over something high, for when they would pull and jerk I could feel it rubbing my neck.
>
> After again refusing to accede to their requests, they forced me to pray. While I was praying, somebody kept continually tugging on the rope.

The judge was pushed down on his knees for the prayer. Perhaps the crowd expected the prayer to be a plea for mercy. It was not. One report said he asked that "justice be done" and another report said he only promised "to do the fair thing to all men to the best of my knowledge."

Rosburg said, "The judge prayed that farmers would get better prices and not lose our farms." Rosburg added, "Anyway, I gave the judge a little kick. I said come on get up, you don't mean it anyhow. We really didn't give him much chance to start praying. I said whisky and prayers don't go together anyhow."

A farmer put the truck hubcap on Bradley's head during the prayer and the oil and grease ran down on his face. Somebody took the judge's hand and forced him to smear the grease around his face and head. Others threw sand and dirt in his hair.

One farmer later said with admiration, "When you've got a rope around your neck and your feet start coming off the ground and you don't crack, you've got nerve. They didn't mean to hurt him, but when you get a bunch of fellows sore, anything can happen. The judge had more guts than anybody I ever saw."

After the prayer, the judge reportedly took an oath to serve justice faithfully (which he would have done under any circumstances) and the mob scattered.

One description said the ashen judge was a lonely figure with his lips showing traces of blood where he had been struck and with his neck showing marks from the rope. He was covered with grime and dirt.

Several farmers (evidently not the attackers) offered to take Bradley back to town. He refused the offers, then allowed Wilbur DePree, son of a clergyman, to drive him to the courthouse.

Judge Bradley went into his office and asked to be left alone.

He told newsmen, "I don't think I can say anything tonight, boys."

Governor Herring immediately declared martial law in Plymouth County and adjacent territory, meaning O'Brien County, scene of the Primghar riot.

National Guard units reached the area the next day and started making arrests in town and out in the country. By May 6, the Guard had taken 45 farmers into custody at Primghar and 47 at Le Mars.

Rosburg and Cope fled. Rosburg returned after a couple of weeks and was arrested by Rippey. Cope went to Minnesota, where he worked by the day. He was gone 11 weeks and was taken into custody when he got back.

Cope, Rosburg and one Clyde Casper all received six-month sentences in the county jail for assault with intent to do great bodily injury. They each served three months. Governor Herring suspended the final three months.

Among the other defendants, Lawrence Krause went to jail for 42 days but said he didn't mind it: "I wasn't married." John Sokolovske was jailed for 30 days and didn't like it at all: "Being in jail taught me plenty." A.A. Mitchell, the only farmer to stand trial, was convicted in a hearing at Orange City and given a 30-day sentence. He was accused of providing the half-inch rope that went around Judge Bradley's neck.

The abuse of the judge is a bad dream in Iowa history. The mob action had unreal qualities the day it happened. Rome Starzl, editor of the *Le Mars Globe Post,* was on the scene:

> We watched the faces of the crowd surrounding the milling nucleus of the mob. Many of them wore queerly frightened expressions. Everywhere were pale grins and anxious eyes.
>
> Even some of those who were actively handling the judge seemed strange, moving about like auto mans [automatons], or like self-conscious actors who knew many eyes were on them. Their eyes sought approval and mutual support.
>
> One gathered that this business was distasteful to them but they were impelled by a destiny they could not resist. Experts in crowd psychology might explain it. We have seen birds do the same thing—set upon some unlucky individual and sometimes kill it, for no valid reason. It must be some form of madness.

The attack drew widespread condemnation. A *Des Moines Register* editorial said, "The great, the overwhelming majority of Iowa's farmers disapprove of such actions by men pretending to represent the farmers' interests."

The Plymouth County Bar Association commended Bradley's "courageous refusal to comply with the illegal and insulting demands made on him while he was in a helpless and desperate situation, in the hands of a mob of unthinking and irresponsible persons. We denounce all such demonstrations as a gross misrepresentation to the country at large of the people of this community, of those engaged in farming."

In defense of farmers generally, the *Le Mars Sentinel* said that less than 10 percent of Plymouth County farmers had been active in the Holiday movement. The *Sentinel* recalled that a Holiday group had threatened Judge Pitts in his office earlier in the year and had gotten away with it. "That successful defiance of authority," the newspaper said, "made easier their attack on Judge Bradley and their participation in the clash at Primghar."

Sheriff Rippey found himself a storm center after the attack. First reports said Rippey was at home in the jail at the corner of the courthouse yard during the disturbance. He was quoted as saying he hadn't slept in three nights and "I had gone upstairs to sleep a bit." He was said to have given orders not to be disturbed. Phone calls went unanswered.

Those reports upset a lot of people, including Governor Herring. "If Sheriff Rippey hadn't been such a weak sister," the governor said, "all this wouldn't have happened."

Rippey heatedly denied the accuracy of the reports.

"I was not in Le Mars at all that day but had gone to Des Moines to confer with Herring about the need for remedial farm legislation," the sheriff said. "I stressed the urgency of the situation, that things were getting out of control since all livestock from the north and east was channeled through Le Mars to Sioux City and we had become a focal point and battleground for the pickets."

Rippey said he didn't get home until evening, after it was all over. He said Herring wrote a letter apologizing for the "weak sister" remark. Judge Bradley also defended Rippey and the people of Plymouth County gave the sheriff a vote of confidence the next year by re-electing him.

But the question remained: Why did Herring say such a thing

if he met with Rippey that day in Des Moines, well over 200 miles from Le Mars? And why wasn't Herring's apology printed in the newspapers?

Another question. The rioters themselves admitted they had been drinking before the Primghar attack and before they grabbed the judge. Where did they get the liquor? Prohibition was still in effect and liquor was illegal. Rippey provided an explanation. He said a Sioux City bootlegger had equipped a number of farmers with liquor distilling equipment. They made whisky in their hog houses, an activity that was more profitable than raising hogs. The bootlegger bought the whisky for distribution in Sioux City and elsewhere in northwest Iowa.

Leading participants in the Bradley violence were not happy afterwards with what they had done. Yet they believed they had performed a distinct service to farmers everywhere by calling the nation's attention to the plight of agriculture.

"I ain't sorry," Rosburg declared. "But we shouldn't have taken the judge out there. We were crazy to do that."

Rosburg added, "We still claim us Holiday fellows woke up the big shots to do something for the farmer. What happened before will never happen again."

Cope commented, "Our trouble forced the people in the east to look this far west to see what was happening. It all helped. I thought it did good. What we wanted was the cost of production." Cope had suffered plenty himself from low prices. He had sold hogs as low as $2.65 per 100 pounds in 1932.

Cope hung on through the 1930s and recovered in a big way in the 1940s from the ravages of the Depression. He was an excellent livestock feeder and he made a lot of money as prices shot up during World War II and afterwards. He told of getting as much as $39 per 100 pounds for cattle and $28.50 for hogs, tremendous prices for the times. It was said that one Holidayer did so well in later years that he was able to lose $18,000 investing in oil stock without going broke.

An additional casualty in the courtroom attack was Scott Reiniger, Bradley's shorthand reporter. Scott was sitting at his desk looking at the judge when the rioters rushed by. A farmer walloped Scott on the right jaw, knocking him to the floor. His only discernible injury was a big lump on the jaw, so prominent that when he went home his wife accused him of chewing tobacco, which of course he wasn't.

Judge Bradley never expressed anger toward his tormentors. In fact, he expressed sympathy for them. "I am something of a farmer myself," he said, "in that I hold considerable property myself and I realize full well the problems farmers are up against." He resigned from the district bench in December 1933 to accept appointment as trustee of the Royal Union Life Insurance Company assets in Des Moines. He died of a stroke in 1939 at 60 years of age.

The rural strife didn't go away at all after the Bradley ordeal. A major riot broke out near Denison, Iowa, the next day.

A Roaring Battle

S heriff Hugo Willey thought he was ready for big trouble in Depression-plagued Crawford County.

He wasn't.

Farmer Joseph F. Shields, who lived near the county seat town of Denison, had gone broke. He couldn't pay $1,400 rent he owed landlord Louis Houlihan.

Willey held an auction April 28, 1933, in the farmer's barnyard to sell off his movable assets and pay Houlihan. The sheriff brought along 30 deputies and six agents of the State Bureau of Investigation to safeguard the sale. The deputies were armed with wagon wheel spokes and pickaxe handles. At least one agent carried a gun.

More than 1,000 tense farmers and others converged on the Shields place. One farmer wanted to address the crowd and ask that nobody bid full value on items in the auction. Willey wouldn't let him speak. The sheriff advised the big gathering that any disturbance would lead to postponement of the sale, which would then be held at a later time under martial law.

The auction appeared to go smoothly at first. Willey sold one pile of corn at 20 cents a bushel and a second pile at 22½ cents.

As a third pile was being sold, "a flying wedge of 800 farmers" charged into the ring. Officers swung clubs wildly but were overwhelmed.

"They were thrown to the ground, kicked and some were jumped on," said one report. "Farmers also fell as sticks, fists and brickbats flew. The fighting mob, surrounded by a ring of spectators that brought the crowd to 1,200, surged back and forth in the farm yard between two big barns.

"No holds were barred as the farmers and their opponents alike kicked and scratched, gouged, sometimes on their feet, as often rolling on the ground."

Willey said the charge was led by "100 very hostile men in the wedge who were joined by another 100 men in the fight."

Three agents were severely beaten. Agent Marion Stevens said:

> I saw the fight start with a flying human wedge which came into the sale ring with the force of a tractor behind a snow plow. As I turned around, four or five fellows grabbed me and somebody socked me over the head with a billy. I was blinded for three or four minutes. Somebody had taken the billy off my arm and others grabbed my gun from its holster before I went out.

Stevens succeeded in wrenching back the gun. When he regained his sight, he said, half a dozen men had ganged up on him, hit him on the side of the head, cut his lip and choked him. A farmer told him, "Get your bunch and get out of here damn quick!"

The attackers threw Jack Hess, a special deputy from Schleswig, Iowa, into a water tank. Others threatened to hang L.V. Gilchrist, attorney for landlord Houlihan. Stevens said it would have taken "riot guns" to control the crowd.

The conflict finally died down, with a lot of bruised bodies and heads but apparently no serious injuries. Willey called out in the middle of the melee postponing the sale but nobody heard him.

That same day Iowa Governor Clyde L. Herring declared martial law in Crawford County and ordered National Guard troops to the scene. The Guardsmen had a tough task to perform upon arrival. They had to oust a milling crowd of 700 farmers from the courthouse in Denison.

The next day the sheriff completed the sale at the Shields farm. There were no interruptions for two good reasons: Guardsmen posted machine guns aimed at the crowd and searched everybody for weapons before admitting them to the farmyard.

The Guard also went looking for rioters and placed at least 63 individuals under arrest. Twenty-two pleaded guilty when taken to court in Denison. They got off easy considering the seriousness of the offense. Each was fined $50 and sentenced to one day in jail.

Cornfield Prophet

H enry Agard Wallace was walking with friends in Des Moines' Waterworks Park one winter afternoon when his world suddenly changed forever.

A Western Union messenger found the party and delivered a telegram to Henry. It was from Franklin D. Roosevelt, president-elect of the United States.

Roosevelt offered the post of Secretary of Agriculture to Wallace. Henry sent an immediate wire of acceptance. The date was Feb. 26, 1933.

Thus was Henry A. Wallace of Des Moines launched on a career that included eight years in the president's cabinet (1933-1941); four years as vice president of the United States (1941-1945); one year plus as Secretary of Commerce (1945-1946) and an abortive third-party candidacy for president in 1948.

Thus also was the way paved for Wallace to become a prime architect of the sweeping New Deal farm programs that committed billions of dollars annually to bolstering farm income through such measures as price supports, crop loans, reduced production, set-aside acres and soil conservation.

The New Deal instituted this vast course of action for the purpose of solving an enormous national economic problem. Agriculture in 1933 was in a state of virtual collapse as the culmination of a farm depression that started after the end of the 1914-1918 World War I.

On the day that Wallace got the telegram, the *Des Moines Register* reported that corn futures on the Chicago market had declined to the lowest levels since 1897, with May corn at 24 ½ cents a bushel. The newspaper said cash corn was bringing a disastrous 13½ to 14 cents a bushel in Des Moines.

In accepting the cabinet post, Henry left his job as editor of the widely read farm paper *Wallaces' Farmer,* published in Des Moines.

Not only had Henry been a fighting farm editor. He was a longtime successful corn breeder as well. He launched what became Pioneer Hi-Bred International of Des Moines, a dominant world seed corn company.

Vital though his contributions were to agriculture through the New Deal, Henry's role in the spectacular increase in corn production may have been even more important. He did not discover hybrids nor was he the only corn experimenter. But a leading plant scientist wrote: "Henry A. Wallace, more than any other single individual, introduced hybrid corn to the American farmer and fervently promoted its adoption."

Prior to hybrids, Iowa farmers harvested a state average of 38 to 40 bushels of corn to the acre. That average has soared above 125 bushels to the acre in good years since, and reached a record 147 bushels in 1992. Other states and nations showed like increases. It was a great scientific and economic advance for mankind.

Wallace was one of Des Moines' most successful businessmen ever. He made a number of individuals rich as well as himself and family in the Pioneer company. He enjoyed an income of well beyond $100,000 annually in years when the dollar had a lot more value than at present. (Des Moines was his home or legal residence for half a century, from the late 1890s until 1949.)

At the same time, the many-sided Henry was a devout Bible student and a strange mystic who delved into Far Eastern religions. And he sought in the late 1940s to accommodate to Soviet communism in his quest for world peace.

Even so, Wallace sensed better than any of his era that the Soviet system would eventually collapse. In 1963, a quarter century before the fact, he said the Soviets "must realize within 20 years that Russia can survive only by throwing in her lot with the west." He added: "Sooner or later Russia will understand that longtime self interest demands that she stop her destructive leadership of the common man."

Which is exactly what happened in the Soviet Union in the early 1990s, to the astonishment of the Central Intelligence Agency (CIA), the president, and Congress and the United Nations.

Henry Agard Wallace established a record of sorts by following in the footsteps of his father into a presidential cabinet. His dad, Henry Cantwell Wallace, was Secretary of Agriculture from 1921 until his death in 1924. Father-and-son service in the cabinet is at least unusual in American history and never happened before or since in the agriculture post. The politics of the two Wallaces were different too. Henry Cantwell was an appointee of Republican President Warren Harding. Henry Agard broke with the Republican leadership and became a bulwark of the Democratic Roosevelt administration.

Roosevelt was on a cruise with his advisers in the Caribbean that February 1933 Sunday, preparing a list of appointees to take with him into office on the March 4 inauguration day.

At the same time, Henry Wallace was having Sunday dinner in Des Moines with three friends: Jay Tone, head of the Tone Spices Company; and Fred Lehmann, Jr., and William F. Riley, both well-known Des Moines attorneys.

"The dinner was at either Tone's or Riley's," Lehmann said many years later. "Afterward we all went for a walk in Waterworks Park at the foot of the 28th Street hill. A Western Union boy found us. He had orders to keep after us until he found us and he was a good boy. He did."

Lehmann said the telegram "had traveled by several different routes from the ship to shore and across the country to reach us as we walked in the park."

Wallace had been prominently mentioned for some time as a possible agricultural choice. But Lehmann said: "I think Henry was as surprised as any of us. The talk had been that [Henry] Morgenthau would be given the job but he was switched to Secretary of the Treasury."

Roosevelt acted fast after receiving the Wallace response. The president-elect announced the appointment late that same day.

Genuine enthusiasm greeted the Wallace choice in Des Moines and Iowa. Dante Pierce, publisher of *Wallaces' Farmer,* proudly changed the masthead of his paper to read: "Henry A. Wallace, editor, on leave of absence as Secretary of Agriculture."

The *Des Moines Tribune* said:

> President Roosevelt has given a gratifying indication to American farmers that he has serious intentions about farm

relief by his appointment of Henry A. Wallace.

For neither the farm population nor the President-elect himself can have the slightest reason for thinking that Mr. Wallace goes into that office for any other purpose than to get results.

His integrity and devotion to the farm cause are simply not questioned, and that is a tremendous asset. When it is coupled with ability and determination—which means enough good healthy stubbornness to do what has been categorically promised—it ought to be very encouraging.

Charles E. Hearst, president of the Iowa Farm Bureau Federation, said the appointment met with the "universal approval of the farmers of Iowa. My personal friendship with his grandfather, his father and himself convinces me of his fitness for the position."

Wallace said: "I hope I can bring to my job the same energy and courage which my father demonstrated when he was Secretary of Agriculture under Harding." Then with a crack at Presidents Harding and Calvin Coolidge, who succeeded Harding, Henry added: "I have an advantage in my chief that my father did not have. I will have the privilege of working under a leader who is definitely progressive and entirely sympathetic toward agriculture."

Henry said he would do his very best in Washington and "when it is over I'll come back home." But he never did return to live in Des Moines.

Henry A. Wallace was 44 years old when he took office in Washington. He was a studious, boyish, somewhat shy individual, a brown-haired, blue-eyed 170-pounder who stood 5 feet 10 inches tall. He was a non-drinker, non-smoker who stayed in good physical condition. He played tennis, walked four miles a day, did some boxing at times and threw a boomerang frequently.

Apparently his only major health problem prior to his final illness was a bout with tuberculosis in 1916 when he was 28 years old. He spent some time recuperating in the Colorado Rockies and staged a full recovery.

Henry was born October 7, 1888, near Orient, Iowa, on a farm operated by his father. The family moved in a few years to Ames, where father Wallace joined the faculty of Iowa State College (now Iowa State University) as a dairy professor.

HENRY A. WALLACE in Iowa City

The family moved again in 1896 to Des Moines when Henry was 7. His father became an editor on *Wallaces' Farmer,* founded that year by "Uncle Henry" Wallace, the patriarch of the family and Henry A.'s grandfather. Sturdy Christian "Uncle Henry," a former Presbyterian preacher, adopted this motto for the paper: "Good Farming, Clear Thinking, Right Living."

The inspiration and instruction Henry A. received as a boy from his elders helped make him the topflight human being and dedicated researcher that he was. One student of Henry A. wrote: "The story of Wallace's corn breeding work must start with his childhood. Instilled in him was an almost insatiable thirst for knowledge, especially with regard to plants. This he attributed in part to George Washington Carver."

Carver, the famed black agricultural chemist and inventor, obtained his bachelor's degree at Iowa State in 1894 and his master's in 1896. Henry was 6 and 7 years old when Carver took him on long walks and explained the various types of plants they observed in the countryside.

Carver said the lad had a "precocious ability" in the study of plant life. Wallace told Carver years later his characterization wasn't true "but your flattery induced me to become intensely interested in growing plants."

Also, Henry's mother wanted him to become interested in various forms of life and "above all in plants." When he was 8, she supervised him in a successful cross-breeding of African violets.

Henry's specific interest in corn was sharpened in 1902 when *Wallaces' Farmer* opened a campaign to improve the seed of that crop. The practice had been for the farmer to go to the corn crib in the spring, pick out good-looking ears and plant that seed.

In their positions as editors interpreting farm life, "Uncle" Henry and Henry C. felt there had to be a better way to get dependable seed of high productivity.

Young Henry A. was 13 years old at the time and well able to comprehend the family conversation and the writings about the campaign. And land was available as a laboratory right in Des Moines for teen-age Henry to work the soil himself.

"My first real acquaintance with growing things came when my father bought a dilapidated old house and 10 acres of land at 38th Street and University Avenue," Henry said. "This was in 1899 when I first learned to milk a cow and take care of a sow and her pigs. The house [which was at 38th and Cottage Grove, now the site of the Grace Methodist Church] had slanting floors and cracked linoleum floor covering. The plumbing was out of doors and the barn was ramshackle." Not many comforts of civilization were available in the home on Des Moines' west side, in an area long since built up.

"Between University and Cottage Grove we grew sorghum for the cows and put it in shocks," he recalled. "The winter snow would make it hard for me to pull the sorghum stalks free. Of course there was no city water and no electric lights. My sister Annabelle would hold the lantern while I fed and milked the cows."

High school wasn't all that much fun either.

"Going to West High at 15th and Center two miles away was

not an especially joyous time for me," Henry said. "I had to walk four miles a day, take care of two cows and for a time do a lot of water pumping."

But things looked up: "After my father bought a Maxwell automobile, then a Glide and then a Franklin, and capped it all by joining a country club, I suddenly woke up to the fact that there might be something more to life than hard work."

Of major importance to all the Wallaces in this period was the arrival at Iowa State College from Illinois of Perry G. Holden. Professor Holden has been described as "one of the most magnetic and inspirational leaders in promoting better methods in agricultural production."

Holden staged corn shows and traveled the state in a "corn train" to interest farmers in seeking better seed.

In 1904 16-year-old Henry and his father attended a Holden short course at Ames on how to judge corn ears individually and in collections of 10 ears. Young Henry sat for a long time judging samples under the watchful eye of a corn judge. The youth came away stimulated and impressed by Holden's keen perception and his ability to inspire his listeners.

Nevertheless, the budding researcher in Henry A. refused to accept the judgments of the time on seed corn. Raymond F. Baker, later a longtime business associate of Henry A., told of a show where farmers entered their corn ears in competition.

> Holden selected for first prize the most uniform sample with all the ears having uniform straight rows and uniform color and size. Young Wallace questioned why the pretty ear sample was actually the most productive. Holden said it was just natural those large beautiful ears would produce a high percent of good ears.

Wallace asked for actual data.

"Holden had none," Baker said. "He suggested that young Henry select some of the smaller, less uniform ears. Farmers called them nubbins."

Upon Holden's suggestion, Henry conducted a field test. He planted alternate rows of seeds from prize ears and from nubbins.

In the fall "young Henry harvested the ears from each row and weighed them," Baker said. "To the surprise of everyone except Wallace, the crop produced from the nubbins out yielded the rows from the prize ears. This convinced Wallace that the looks of an ear of corn were not correlated with yield."

It was about this same time that teen-age Henry negotiated his first commercial corn venture.

"The first real money I ever earned was in the fall of 1904 when I sold 10 bushels of seed corn for $50," he said. "This corn was produced on five acres which I had planted by hand between Cottage Grove and University and between what is now 38th and 39th streets. I had detasseled plants."

He was on the road to becoming perhaps the world's greatest exponent of hybrid corn in his time.

Henry got a lot out of the four years, from 1906 to 1910, that he spent at Iowa State College. He crossed corn plants as a freshman. He continued his search for topflight corn seeds and trained himself as well as a statistician and a forecaster of corn and meat trends. He wrote his first contribution to *Wallaces' Farmer* in 1907, describing his earlier finding that the appearance of an ear of corn had no relation to its productivity. Anyway, he mused, "what are looks (of an ear of corn) to a hog?" He was 19 years old at the time.

Henry's passion for learning didn't end with graduation and with going to work on *Wallaces' Farmer*. He spent a lot of time studying in the Des Moines public library after his college days and he took courses at Drake University as well. His quest for more and more education lasted all his life.

One of his early useful projects (1915) was development of a statistical method under which the farmer could figure the ratio between what it cost him in corn and other expenses to produce a hog and what the animal brought in the market, called the "corn-hog ratio" now. Many farmers had only a dim idea of how they were doing from a cost of production standpoint.

Devout Henry found the Bible economically useful. In a 1912 article, he recalled the Old Testament story of the Pharaoh who dreamed he saw seven fat cattle eaten by seven skinny ones. Joseph, the son of Jacob, told the Pharaoh the dream meant Egypt would have seven years of good crops followed by seven years of famine. Joseph suggested that grain be stored in good years to tide the nation over in the predicted bad years. Joseph got the job of arranging the storage.

"Every year somebody must play the part of Joseph," Henry

wrote. "The farmer can hold the grain if he is prepared for it. . . . We shall come to this by and by and the farmers will be prepared to play Joseph simply by holding their grain and refusing to sell in a market glutted with wheat."

Out of this more than a generation later came Wallace's "Ever Normal Granary" plan under which surpluses were stored in heavy production years for use in lean years.

Wallace's religion was undiluted. His knowledge of the Old Testament prophets was extensive: "I like Isaiah and his far-reaching vision," he said, "Jeremiah and his dauntless courage, Micah and his immortal deliniation of man's duty to 'do justly, love mercy and walk humbly.' And Amos. I suppose I am especially fond of Amos." (Amos believed in a fatherhood of God that insisted on social justice for all people, be they rich or poor.)

Wallace called Christ "the greatest liberal of all time when he put life before things, when he said to seek the Kingdom of Heaven first and things would take care of themselves." Henry said what modern Christianity had to do was apply "the spirit of Jesus against the background of 20th century science."

Wallace had no time for those who maintained that man is just a "poor miserable sinner." He declared the church should teach that man "has infinite possibilities when he is armed with the religion of potentialism, instead of being depressed by the religion of guilt and fear." He said: "If I were to draw conclusions from my life, I would say the purpose of existence here on earth is to improve the quality and increase the abundance of joyous living."

Wallace did some moving around among the Christian sects. He inherited the Presbyterian faith of his grandfather (the family attended the Elmwood United Presbyterian Church on 35th Street south of University, long since gone). He left Presbyterianism because of its stern Calvinistic beliefs and first looked into Catholicism before becoming an Episcopalian in 1930.

Henry did considerable moving as well in presidential politics. He voted not on party labels but most of the time on whether a candidate had the interest of the farmer at heart.

The Wallaces were traditionally Republican but in 1912 they all, including Henry A., voted for Theodore Roosevelt, the Progressive candidate for president. Roosevelt lost to Democrat Woodrow Wilson, to the disappointment of the Wallace clan.

Henry A. opposed both Republican Presidents Calvin Coolidge, elected in 1924, and Herbert Hoover, elected in 1928. Henry A. voted in 1924 for Robert LaFollete, the third-party Progressive candidate, and in 1928 for Democrat Al Smith. Henry continued as a Democrat the next 16 years, understandably voting for Franklin Roosevelt all four times that he ran.

In 1948 Wallace assumed the Progressive label in his own presidential candidacy. And afterwards he surprised a lot of people by voting for Republican Dwight Eisenhower for president in both 1952 and 1956. He returned to the Democratic fold by voting for John F. Kennedy in 1960 and for Lyndon Johnson in 1964.

Conflicts between the Wallaces and their farm paper on one side and national Republican leaders on the other were part of the great agricultural struggle in the years between the 1914-1918 World War I and the New Deal.

The first real clash took place in 1919 when Herbert Hoover was completing his service as national food administrator. Hoover at that time opposed removing the wartime controls that held down prices farmers received for hogs and wheat. Henry A. maintained the farmer was entitled to uncontrolled higher prices. But Wallace didn't condemn Hoover altogether. Henry said: "In these instances he [Hoover] was acting as a friend of the consumer, which was to his credit, but not as a friend of the farmer."

The hog controls went off anyway and prices shot up in 1919, to the benefit of the farmer. But late the next year, in 1920, came the collapse that plummeted prices of hogs and other commodities to bankruptcy levels. The farm depression, but not yet the great national depression, was under way. The Great Depression came nine years later.

Wallace objected strenuously as well in the 1920s and early 1930s to Republican-sponsored protective tariffs. Such tariffs protected prices of American industrial products by pricing competing foreign-made goods out of the American market. American farm commodities were similarly protected. But the commodities were produced at such low cost in America that the farmer didn't need that protection. At the same time he was forced to pay artificially higher prices for industrial products he had to buy.

"The old idea [that] a protective tariff builds up a better

market is no longer true," Henry wrote. He advised the farmer to seek lower tariffs on industrial goods rather than higher ones on farm products. The family farm, he added, had no way of restricting its competition "as the business world does."

He called the Smoot-Hawley tariff enacted in 1930 "the worst tariff bill ever adopted in the United States." That viewpoint has had a lot of support among economists and historians ever since.

Where Henry disagreed most decisively with the Republicans was over President Coolidge's two vetoes of the McNary-Haugen bill in 1927 and 1928. That bill called for boosting farm prices domestically by purchase of depressing surpluses by a proposed new federal corporation. The corporation then would sell the surpluses at lower world prices on markets abroad. The farmer would shoulder the overall cost by paying a so-called "equalization fee."

Wallace and farm forces ardently supported the plan but Coolidge killed it twice and Hoover opposed it as well. Wallace wrote: "The veto message has made it impossible for any farmer with self-respect to vote for Coolidge or any other candidate who, like Hoover, supports the Coolidge policy toward agriculture."

Hoover was nominated for president in 1928 and Al Smith, governor of New York, was his Democratic opponent. Wallace advised: "I think it would be a fine thing for farmers who are thinking of the welfare of agriculture if they would plunk their votes solidly for Smith." But not many farmers did switch. Hoover won easily, nationally and in Iowa as well.

Hoover was inaugurated March 4, 1929. The next October, seven months later, came the mighty stock market crash of the Great Depression. That month also marked the beginning of the end of Wallace control of *Wallaces' Farmer.*

A deal was completed October 26, 1929, merging *Wallaces' Farmer* with its rival farm publication *The Iowa Homestead,* also of Des Moines. Business manager John P. Wallace, Henry's uncle, negotiated the deal, buying out the *Homestead* from Dante Pierce of Des Moines and assuming a mortgage of more than $2 million.

The merger gave the combined *Wallaces' Farmer* and *Iowa Homestead* a circulation of more than 250,000 and might have proved successful if the Depression hadn't taken such a stranglehold on the economy. Henry was in Europe attending an international agricultural conference at the time. He was against the merger, but there was nothing he could do about it when he got home.

The paper fought hard to stay solvent the next three years but couldn't make it. The mortgage burden was too heavy. *Wallaces' Farmer-Iowa Homestead* was forced into receivership in 1932. The Dante Pierce interests took over the publication.

The year 1932 was grim in Iowa and the nation, the grimmest since the Civil War in many ways. President Hoover faced certain defeat in his bid for re-election that fall. Henry A. Wallace, who stayed on as *Wallaces' Farmer-Homestead* editor, staged on all-out attack on Hoover and the Republicans before the election.

> Starving the farmers out is one way to reduce acreage and reduce production. It is the method followed in the last 12 years. So far as we can tell, it is the only method the Republican leadership plans for the next four years.
> The only thing to vote for in this election is justice for agriculture. With Roosevelt the farmers have a chance, with Hoover none. I shall vote for Roosevelt.

The Roosevelt landslide followed and propelled Henry Wallace into the nation's top agriculture post.

Henry's devoted efforts in the cause of the farmer didn't interfere at all with the intensity of his corn experiments and hybrid studies. He shifted corn breeding activities from the garden at his home at 3821 John Lynde Road in Des Moines to a 40-acre tract near the city.

Wallace had started to concentrate on crossbreeding of inbred strains in 1919. His plan was "to develop as many inbred lines of corn as possible, to test as many possible combinations of these inbreds—to discover the super-cross," said one writer.

"Anything that will increase the yield of corn by even so little as one bushel per acre is tremendously worthwhile," Henry commented. (How far he outstripped that goal!)

Wallace wrote to corn breeders all over the United States (there apparently were quite a few), and to others in Europe, South America and Australia. He asked for seed from their most promising lines to add to the inbreds he long had been developing. He in turn gave freely of his own information and seed.

"At one time or other I have worked with inbreds from nearly every corn experimenter in the United States," he said. "When I started inbreeding work, there was a splendid fellowship prevailing among the different experimenters and some of us at least felt it was mutually advantageous to exchange inbreds."

Henry had developed more than 100 inbreds by 1923 and had approximately 800 such lines ready to plant by the spring of 1925.

In 1923 he perfected a variety he called "Copper Cross" corn, so named because of its queer reddish color. This corn, of twin parentage of unusual hybrids, won a gold medal for yield in the 1924 Iowa corn contest.

"Copper Cross" was history's first commercial hybrid. Fifteen bushels were sold for $1 a pound, or $840 total.

Wallace scored a further success in that same contest when an entry from the U.S. Department of Agriculture won a first with a yield 30 percent higher than a top open-pollinated variety. One of the two USDA entries' parents was a Wallace product.

Another major victory was recorded in state contest results announced in 1928. Raymond Baker, then a young associate, and Wallace entered several hybrids.

"The results couldn't have been better," Baker said. "Baker and Wallace won two gold medals, a bronze medal and the banner trophy, a silver cup for the grand champion."

The inbred work was a major part of the everyday life of the Wallace family. Baker told of going to the Wallace home with his wife for a Sunday dinner.

"After dinner Henry and I retired to Wallace's basement where he kept his inbreds," Baker said. "He showed me each one like a proud father and described in detail their good points and weaknesses."

All the while Wallace promoted hybrid corn in the columns of the farm paper. He said he "poured tons of printer's ink" into the subject into the paper and "greatly hastened the adoption of hybrid corn."

In 1926 he launched the Hi-Bred Corn Company (later Pioneer Hi-Bred). Joining him in the enterprise were his brother James W.; his attorney, Fred Lehmann, Jr.; J.J. Newlin, a tenant on a Wallace farm in Johnston; and Simon Casady, a close friend and fellow experimenter.

It was hard going to begin with. Hi-Bred lost $1,235 in the 1927 fiscal year and showed a combined profit of only $17,000 the first six years. It was difficult to get a farmer to pay $12.50 for a bushel of seeds when he had been getting what he needed at no cost from his own crib.

Baker wanted a job with the company but said it was "operating on a shoestring with no salaried employees." Newlin was general manager and received only commissions on the seed he sold. Newlin finally hired Baker as a farmhand for $60 a month "and a gallon of milk a day."

The firm grew slowly and didn't gain wide approval until after drought-stricken 1936. Iowa farmers planted only 5 percent hybrids that year and Illinois farmers little more than 3 percent. But the hybrids yielded twice as much as open-pollinated corn. The average Iowa yield in 1936 was a devastating 17.7 bushels to the acre. But where an open-pollinated yield was 20 bushels, a hybrid field nearby was likely to have yielded 40 bushels. Word spread fast. By 1938 half the Iowa plantings and 59 percent of those in Illinois were hybrids. The Wallace company profits soared from $59,000 in 1936 to $151,000 in 1937 to $321,000 in 1938. Pioneer was off and running.

The Wallaces owned a considerable portion of the company of course, although Henry's personal holdings were not that great. He owned only 68.6 of the 2,000 shares outstanding. His wife Ilo was the largest single shareholder with 754 shares. Henry also had a contract giving him 10 percent of the profits.

As Pioneer was slowly beginning to stir, the New Deal for agriculture under Wallace was gaining considerable acceptance in rural America. Federal corn loans put badly needed cash into farmers' pockets. The loan of 45 cents a bushel was about 20 or 22 cents higher than the market, and farmers were allowed to repay the debt with cheap corn instead of money.

Payment to farmers to take land out of production also was generally well received. That program was designed to handle burdensome surpluses of staples such as wheat, corn, cotton, rice and tobacco. Another major goal was to preserve the soil for future generations by planting legumes (grass, clover, alfalfa) instead of row crops on erosion-vulnerable acres.

Payments were made as well to cut output of hogs and milk. Farm income rose more than 30 percent in 1935 over 1932.

But the inevitable complexities created plenty of problems for

Wallace. The program wasn't for everybody in agriculture, nor could it be. Mostly it was designed originally for the staple products from average and large farms. The small farmer, the sharecropper, felt it didn't do much for him. The courts shot down important parts of the system. Henry came under fire frequently, as have nearly all secretaries since.

Specific problems developed. The program was to have been paid for by proceeds of a processing tax. The Supreme Court declared that tax levied on the marketing of farm products unconstitutional. It didn't work as expected anyway. The hog farmer found that what he got from the packer for his animals was reduced by the amount of the tax the packer paid, which the farmer didn't like at all.

Wallace also heard plenty from critics when he ordered the purchase and destruction of six million baby pigs to strengthen future pork prices. Pointing out that the pigs ultimately would have been slaughtered for food, Henry commented: "We didn't raise them as pets."

Furthermore, the New Deal program didn't lower grain production as much as it was supposed to. Farmers themselves were largely to blame. They took their marginal land out of production as planned, but they heavily fertilized their good acres and produced bumper crops that hurt prices and offset the acreage cuts to a considerable extent.

Fortunately for the program, but not for the afflicted farmers, devastating droughts hit the Midwest in 1934 and 1936. Iowa's 1934 corn yield dropped to 28.2 bushels to the acre, against a normal of 38 to 40, and to only 17.7 bushels in 1936. Prices rose sharply, from 35 cents a bushel in 1933 to 90 cents in 1934 to $1.03 in 1936.

Wasn't Wallace inconsistent in cutting corn production while promoting increased output at the same time through hybrid seed? Henry appears never to have tackled that question head on. He did insist on boosting the farmer's income through reduction of production. He didn't, however, expect hybrids to catch on for many years to come. He thought there would be an interim in which a long-range program could be developed to protect farm income.

There wasn't much of an interim. As previously noted, a

major speedup in use of hybrids took place as a result of the 1936 drought.

The coming of World War II to Europe in 1939 and to the United States and Asia in 1941 pushed agriculture into an era of record prosperity. The emphasis was changed from cutting output to producing as much as possible to feed the war-torn world. That was beginning to happen when Wallace stepped down as Secretary of Agriculture.

Roosevelt selected Henry for the nomination for vice president in the 1940 convention. A lot of delegates opposed Wallace, in part because he was a onetime Republican. The president insisted, however, and Wallace survived and was elected along with Roosevelt. Henry took over his new office in 1941. He had given his all to the farm cause. He left behind a farm program structure that continued to operate for generations.

The vice president position put Henry almost within reach of the presidency in late 1944 and early 1945. Here's what happened: Wallace did not get renominated for vice president by the 1944 Democratic convention. Senator Harry Truman of Missouri replaced Henry on the ticket. Franklin Roosevelt easily won re-election as president in 1944 even though he was a dying man. The president did die April 12, 1945, less than three months after his January 20 inaugural. Had Roosevelt died several months earlier—and he had been in poor condition quite a while—Wallace would have assumed the presidency, at least briefly. Or if Henry had been renominated, he would have become president instead of Truman.

The plain fact was that Roosevelt dumped Wallace from the 1944 ticket. Mayor Ed Kelly, the Democratic boss of Chicago and Roosevelt ally, gave the reason. He said Roosevelt felt he needed more diverse appeal in 1944, that Roosevelt and Wallace drew support from the same groups and that Truman brought additional voters to the ticket.

It also was likely that Wallace's failure as a vote getter in 1940 helped lead to his being discarded. Roosevelt hoped that Henry would help him carry the farm belt in 1940. In fact, Wallace was unable to prevent even his home state of Iowa from going Republican. And Roosevelt lost such farm states as North and South Dakota, Nebraska, Kansas and Indiana as well.

Though Wallace did get knocked off the 1944 ballot, he didn't go easily. His many friends came to the fore in a big way when the

Democrats met in convention in Chicago. He declared: "I am in this fight to the finish."

Even though he was being junked, Wallace delivered a strong speech seconding the Roosevelt renomination for president. "The future," Henry said, "belongs to those who go down unswervingly for the liberal principles of both political democracy and economic democracy, regardless of race, color and religion." He added that the Democrats "cannot long survive as a conservative party."

Henry's appearance on the convention platform touched off a huge demonstration with delegates chanting "We want Wallace! We want Wallace!" Observers believed that Henry would have captured the vice presidential nomination right then and there if the balloting had begun at that point. But the chairman, sensing a possible steamroller, arbitrarily adjourned the convention till the next day, despite a loud majority of "no!" votes from the delegates.

Wallace remained relatively strong the next morning too, and it took some finagling to beat him. Truman strategists persuaded 13 favorite-son candidates to stay in the race, at least for the first ballot. Wallace led on that ballot with 429½ votes to Truman's 319½. The favorite sons received a combined total of 393½. A lot of favorite sons went over to Truman on the second ballot, and he won.

Roosevelt appointed Wallace Secretary of Commerce as a consolation prize in February 1945. Truman unfairly removed Henry from that job in September 1946. Wallace had angered the State Department with a speech charging the department with being too anti-Soviet in foreign relations. Henry had cleared the speech with Truman first but the president nevertheless fired him anyway after getting the adverse State Department reaction.

The period from 1945 to 1950 saw Henry A. Wallace pretty much eliminated as a national and international political force. It was a shadowy part of his life in which, among other things, he was labelled a Communist or at best a fellow traveller, and a kook as well. He was none of these things but years had to pass before those impressions faded.

The Wallace comedown began with his loss of the vice presidency and then the Commerce Cabinet post.

Once again a private citizen after 13 years in the national spotlight, Wallace decided to run for president himself in 1948 as a third-party candidate. He believed he could build a strong

Progressive party on a program of peace, an accord with the Soviet Union and liberal domestic policies. He hoped for an outpouring of support from farmers, blacks, peace activists, liberals and union labor. Walter Reuther, head of the United Auto Workers (UAW), was Henry's firm ally.

The first test was promising. Wallace forces pulled a major upset in early 1948 in New York's Bronx. With Wallace backing, one Leo Isaacson swamped the regular Democratic Party candidate in a congressional by-election. Isaacson was elected under the banner of the American Labor party. That scared Democrats into believing Wallace himself might draw enough votes away from Truman in the 1948 election to give the presidency to the Republicans.

The Progressives met in a rousing convention that summer in Philadelphia and nominated Wallace as planned. The trouble was, Communists embraced the new party and exercised considerable control. The Communists publicly announced their support and Wallace didn't repudiate them, which proved to be a major mistake.

Henry further damaged his image in his acceptance speech. He declared the United States "can't lose anything by giving up [Germany's Berlin to the Russians] in the search for peace." The American people wanted no part of such kowtowing to the Soviets. The people were fed up with Russian treachery and deceit in international negotiations.

Wallace thus proved to be no factor at all in the 1948 election. Truman won an upset victory over Republican Tom Dewey, 24 million votes to 22 million (303 electoral votes to 189). In third place was Dixiecrat Strom Thurmond with 1,169,000 votes and 38 electoral votes. Wallace finished fourth with 1,157,000 votes and no delegates in the Electoral College. There had been no sizable split of Democratic strength away from Truman.

Henry had worked hard to at least capture his home state of Iowa, but to no avail. Politics was not his forte. He polled a paltry 12,125 votes in the state, against 522,380 for Truman and 484,618 for Dewey.

Wallace was barred on one occasion from holding a rally on the University of Iowa campus in Iowa City. (Campaign meetings were forbidden on the state university campuses at the time.) The rally moved to the city park, where somebody threw eggs but missed Wallace. One egg hit a reporter.

Another development that didn't do Wallace any good was his secret contacts with a "guru," or Hindu religious teacher. Westbrook Pegler, a sardonic syndicated columnist, prodded Henry unmercifully on the "guru" issue. Wallace's interest in the subject was in perfect accord with his lifetime explorations of the world's religions. But voters don't like political leaders fooling around with such offbeat stuff and Wallace was branded as being "woolly-minded," a label that was a long time in going away.

Henry didn't leave the public scene altogether after the 1948 loss. In 1949 he denounced the formation of the North Atlantic Treaty Organization (NATO) as a bulwark against Soviet expansion in western Europe. He said NATO would require the United States to spend $20 billion in military assistance (like $150 billion in 1990 dollars). History appears to have proved Wallace wrong on NATO. It proved to be an effective deterrent against Soviet aggression.

By 1950, however, Henry broke with the Communists completely because of their opposition to U.S. and United Nations participation in the Korean War.

When Henry went to Washington in 1933, his story became part of the history of the nation and the world, and beyond this Des Moines and Iowa perspective. Yet his ties with home continued close through Pioneer and members of the family, and he made news frequently when he came back to Des Moines for political or nostalgic reasons.

The Wallaces kept their residence on John Lynde Road in Des Moines through nearly all their Washington years but finally sold it in 1946. In 1949, after the third-party presidential defeat, Henry and Ilo settled on a 115-acre farm near South Salem, New York.

Why didn't they return to Des Moines? "This is the kind of place I've always wanted since I was a boy," Henry said of the New York farm, and added: "We had pretty much become rooted in the east in the 1930s and 1940s, and also I wanted an eastern base for our company's hybridizing and genetic operations."

Henry spent a lot of time at South Salem, happily working with hybrid strawberries and gladiolus. He also worked with hybrid chickens for the Hy-Line Poultry Farms, then a Pioneer subsidiary.

But Henry didn't confine himself to the farm by any means. He served as editor of the *New Republic* magazine in New York for a time and he did considerable other writing. (He wrote 17 books in his lifetime.) And he enjoyed coming back to Iowa for some speaking as well.

As a young man, Wallace had hailed the coming of highways and electric power for bringing a higher standard of living to the farmer. But by 1962 he had swung over to the other side. He said in a Des Moines speech:

> The automobile, good roads and electricity destroyed the United States I had come to love and understand. . . . I still tend to distrust the values and systems thrust upon us since World War I. Electricity and a thousand and one gadgets are no answer.

The pioneers of the 1880s, he said, "were perhaps just as close or even closer to that answer than we. It may be more difficult to live virtuously and wisely with abundance than scarcity."

How close he kept in touch with the seed corn company affairs was demonstrated in a letter he wrote to Baker in 1965, a few months before he died. Baker had sent word of the success of a hybrid variety numbered 3306.

"I was feeling rather blue when I got up this morning thinking the end was not far away," Henry wrote, "but when I got to thinking about 3306, I felt I just had to live to see [how it would adapt] to the tropical program, the Argentine program and the south Georgia program. Yes, this is about the most exciting letter I have ever received from you."

Henry observed his 77th birthday the following October 7 but he wasn't well. About a year before, he had noticed a paralytic lag in his left leg after a strenuous game of tennis. A slight impairment of speech followed. He took a planned trip anyway to the Dominican Republic. There he worked on a strain of strawberries he hoped would provide the Republic with a cash crop. And, ever out to assist his fellow man, he wanted to help make the Dominicans self-sufficient in food.

The paralysis kept getting worse. Wallace went to Europe to consult experts, to no avail. He returned to the United States and entered the National Institutes of Health (NIH) hospital at

Bethesda, Maryland. His problem by that time had been diagnosed as lateral sclerosis, the incurable disease that killed baseball star Lou Gehrig.

The NIH was engaged in research on the disease. True scientist that he was, Henry kept careful track for the doctors of his symptoms and reactions. He felt he thereby might help find a cure for the ailment, just as his own work with plants had contributed to the welfare of humanity.

Henry lost his ability to speak and to move about. He could take nourishment only through a tube in his throat.

He was taken back to the farm after a couple of weeks. Death came November 18, 1965, in a hospital in nearby Danbury, Connecticut.

Henry Agard Wallace did come home to Iowa in the end. The body was cremated and the ashes returned to Glendale Cemetery in Des Moines.

Wallace left an estate of $840,000, a very substantial sum at the time. That, however, was only a portion of the net worth of the Wallaces. He previously had distributed much of his stock and other assets to his children and other relatives. And many of the assets were in the name of Ilo, the widow, who died in 1981 at 93 years of age.

Henry cautioned in his will: "The [Wallace] family will be strong in so far as it recognizes that there are higher values than monetary values."

His thoughts and vision were ever in wide terms. In one of his last speeches in Des Moines, he said: "We are all part of a great unfolding which operates on an ever vaster scale at an ever greater speed. If reform comes fast enough and wisely enough, there never need be a revolution."

Fire the Women!

W orking wives should be fired forthwith and their jobs given to unemployed married men.

That was the incredible position taken in depression 1933 by Iowa State Labor Commissioner Frank Wenig. Just imagine the feminine wrath that would descend upon his head were he here to take such a stand today. Well over half the married women hold jobs in modern society.

Wenig especially targeted working women whose husbands had jobs. Unemployment reached a horrible 25 percent in the Depression. (Seven percent was looked upon as too high in 1993.)

Census figures showed that 37,000 Iowa married women were employed in the early 1930s. Wenig figured opening that many jobs to men would be a decided help in combatting overall unemployment in the state.

There wasn't much public protest to the Wenig attitude. He said he received lots of support for his position and only one objection. Working married women were out of the ordinary. Women employed by the big insurance companies in Des Moines, for example, were automatically terminated when they got married, and they expected to be.

Sometimes a woman secretly wed and stayed on the job, until the boss found out about it. Then there was hell to pay.

Flora was a young daughter of Fred Claussen, widely known Des Moines insurance man. Fred got Flora a job in the policy loan department of the Central Life Assurance Company in Des Moines. Her pay was $54 a month.

Flora and Lynn W. Easter got married in September 1932 and kept it a secret because they needed the money her job brought in. Lynn wasn't making much either working in a family-owned grocery store in Norwalk. Their combined income for the year 1932 was only $1,000.

The couple took elaborate precautions to keep the marriage news from getting out. They were wed in Fulton, Illinois, across the Mississippi River from Clinton, to keep the *Des Moines Register*'s Iowa News Service from finding out about it and publishing the story. Lynn drove to Fulton on a Friday to get the necessary Illinois license. Flora worked as usual till noon Saturday and took a bus to Cedar Rapids, where Lynn picked her up. They went to Fulton and were married in a minister's home. They had no wedding pictures taken. Said Flora: "All we did was get married."

Seven months later, Fred Wolfinger, secretary of Central Life, called Flora to his office.

"What is your name?" he demanded.

"Mrs. Lynn Easter," she replied forthrightly.

"I didn't think a daughter of Fred Claussen would pull a thing like this," Wolfinger angrily declared, referring to her staying on the job after marriage.

"You leave my father out of this," Flora retorted. "He had nothing to do with it. Do I have to leave now or can I stay till 4:30?"

Wolfinger said it would take some time to get her check and she could stay till 4:30.

(Lynn Easter was to become in later years a highly successful Des Moines businessman. The Easters celebrated their 60th wedding anniversary in September 1992.)

Meanwhile, Labor Commissioner Wenig practiced what he preached. He found two married women on his office staff when he took over in 1933. He fired both.

He tried to get mayors of Iowa cities and local chambers of commerce to join in the campaign against employing married women but apparently few if any did. And the Legislature refused to pass a law providing for mandatory separation of married females from their jobs.

In the late 1930s the question of employing married women in the Legislature itself stirred up some commotion. Several lawmakers hired their own wives as secretaries. That didn't sit well with the "economy twins," State Representatives Leo Hoegh of Chariton and Earl Fishbaugh of Shenandoah, both Republicans. They maintained the jobs should be given to others in those difficult times and not monopolized within legislative families.

Hoegh and Fishbaugh pointed fingers of scorn at fellow representatives with wives working for them. But nothing was ever done about it. Actually, in terms of modern money, not a lot was involved. The secretaries were paid $35 a week, or about $500 for a 100-day session every other year. The lawmakers didn't get rich either. The pay of legislators was $1,000 for a regular session every two years, out of which they had to buy their own stamps for the mail and pay their own living expenses while serving in Des Moines. There was no living expenses allowance for them in those days.

Hoegh tried hard in 1937 to get a bill passed barring employment anywhere in state government of a woman with a husband earning $1,500 or more a year. That wasn't a bad job at the time. Hoegh had found out that 30 percent of the women working for the state were married, 370 out of 1,183. Of the 370, a total of 259 had husbands with jobs. Said Hoegh: "State employment should be spread out to support as many people as possible."

The Representative got a lot of attention but no results. The bill failed.

War Agitators

" T he three most important groups who have been pushing this country toward war," declared Charles A. Lindbergh, "are the British, the Jews and the Roosevelt administration."

The famous flyer made that sweeping accusation September 11, 1941, in Des Moines. The speech touched off a national uproar, especially among Jews.

Lindbergh came to Des Moines as a crusader dedicated to keeping the United States out of World War II, then raging in Europe. He addressed a cheering, booing crowd of 8,000 in the old Coliseum on Locust Street near the Des Moines River. The speech was broadcast over the Mutual Radio Network.

It is doubtful whether any other talk ever delivered in Iowa produced such an explosive reaction coast to coast. It was a major outburst in an angry nationwide battle that had been going on for a couple of years between "isolationists" and "non-isolationists."

The isolationists, under the banner of the "America First Committee," wanted no part of the United States getting into the war under any circumstances. The non-isolationists had come to believe that war might be necessary to overcome the cruel German Nazi dictatorship of Adolf Hitler, whom they regarded as a threat to all democracies.

World War II had started in 1938. Nazi armies overwhelmed France, overran such neutral nations as Holland, Belgium, Denmark and Norway, besides crippling Poland. The outlook was bleak for Great Britain standing alone against the Nazis in western Europe.

Less than three months after the Lindbergh Des Moines appearance, the isolation issue became meaningless. The Japanese, allies of Hitler, bombed Pearl Harbor and precipitated the United States into the war. Lindbergh had failed in his neutrality quest.

Lindbergh's prewar role was totally different from what previously had put him into the public eye. He was the beloved hero of all mankind in 1927 after making the first solo flight from New York to Paris across the Atlantic in a small plane. And the heart of the world had gone out to him and his wife in 1932 when his infant son was kidnapped and murdered.

It was less than a decade later that Lindbergh found himself a storm center because of his attitude toward the impending war. His speech was sponsored by the Des Moines chapter of the America First Committee.

CHARLES A. LINDBERGH
in Des Moines
Courtesy of the Des Moines Register

Incidentally, the Committee gave President Roosevelt equal time that night. The president made a strong "Freedom of the Seas" speech in which he announced the American Navy would "shoot on sight" any German or Italian warships encountered in the Atlantic.

The president's broadcast was relayed in full over loudspeakers to the Coliseum crowd before Lindbergh entered. The audience also observed one minute of silence out of respect for the death of the president's mother, Sara Delano Roosevelt.

In his address, Lindbergh didn't limit himself to singling out the British, Jews and Rooseveltians. "Behind these groups but of less importance," he said, "are a number of capitalists, Anglophiles and intellectuals who believe that their future and the future of mankind depend upon the domination of the British empire.

"Add to these the communistic groups who were opposed to intervention until a few weeks ago and I believe I have named the major war agitators in the country."

In retrospect, it is obvious that future high stakes were in the making even as Lindbergh talked. Hundreds of thousands already had been killed in Europe in the war. Many millions more were to die, including 300,000 Americans, before peace was reached in 1945. (The war took the lives of 8,398 Iowans.) Destruction of cities and equipment and the piling up of debt worldwide were enormous.

For all the charges hurled at him, Lindbergh did express friendly insight into the motives of the British and the Jews. The British, he said, "perfectly understandably want the U.S. in the war on their side. England is in a desperate position.

"If she can draw this country into war, she can shift to our shoulders a large part of the responsibility for waging it and for paying its cost."

But he did accuse the British of waging an extensive propaganda campaign to get the United States into the conflict.

As for the Jews, he said, "it is not difficult to understand their desire for the overthrow of Nazi Germany. The persecution they have suffered would be sufficient to make bitter enemies of any race."

Lindbergh got into the most trouble on the Jews with this statement: "Their greatest danger to this country lies in their ownership and influence in our motion pictures, our press, our radio and our government." In other words, he charged Jews with using movies, the press, radio and influence in Washington to get the nation into the war.

That riled millions around the country but drew loud applause as well as boos in Des Moines.

There were sudden bursts of noise both ways from the crowd during the speech. First mention of the British, Jews and the Washington administration got the greatest reaction, with loud applause drowning out angry booing. And criticism of the Roosevelt administration inspired prolonged cheering and major booing at the same time, plus a lot of chattering and chanting that continued for several minutes.

Lindbergh was perhaps harshest in his treatment of the president:

> The Roosevelt administration has used the war emergency to obtain a third Presidential term for the first time in American history. [Roosevelt won a third term in the 1940 election.] Its members have used the war to add unlimited billions to a debt which is the largest we have ever known.
>
> They have used the war to justify the restriction of Congressional power and the assumption of dictatorial procedures on the part of the President and his appointees.

Despite his sincerity, Lindbergh was vulnerable in his position on two counts, considering the climate of the times. First, his good faith understandably came into question when he went to Berlin in 1938 and was decorated by the German government. That didn't sit well with a lot of people.

Then, none of the Lindbergh fire in the speech was directed at Hitler. An editorial in the *Des Moines Register* said:

> The drift of the United States closer to war since 1939 was attributed in no degree [by Lindbergh] to Hitler and his policies and successes, in no degree to the events such as the invasions of innocent neutrals and the terrifying collapse of France. It was attributed wholly to the crafty plotting of three sets of individuals, including the President of the United States.

The *Register* agreed that nearly all Jews were anti-Hitler but said so were a big majority of all Americans. "To single out the Jews was the most irresponsible and deplorable thing that could be done," the newspaper said, and added that the speech had "all the essential elements of Nazi propaganda."

The *San Francisco Chronicle* said: "The voice is the voice of Lindbergh but the words are the words of Hitler." And the *New York Herald Tribune* declared Lindbergh had "departed from the American way [with] an unmistakable appeal to anti-Semitism."

It appeared that Lindbergh had plenty of supporters as well as detractors in Iowa at the time. Certainly there were plenty of both at the Coliseum that night.

Some of his backers were prominent Iowans. He was introduced by Robert Bannister, well-known Des Moines attorney, who called Lindbergh "an American, a patriot who is unafraid."

Even more notable a supporter was Hanford MacNider of

Mason City, a highly decorated Purple Heart veteran of World War I. MacNider also had been Minister to Canada, national commander of the American Legion, an Iowa favorite-son candidate for vice president and onetime superior of Dwight Eisenhower when both were in the War Department in Washington. In a strong speech at the Lindbergh meeting, MacNider declared:

> I am not for condemning every future generation of Americans to die policing the whole world. Our youngsters' lives and their freedom mean more to me than keeping the world safe for communism and Joe Stalin, than freeing Europe from Hitler or any other dictator.
>
> Our best contribution to a sorely troubled world, and the only real contribution we can make, is to maintain this land of ours as a great citadel of enlightened democracy to which men can repair for guidance and inspiration.

On the other side and bitterly opposed to Lindbergh was a Des Moines "Fight for Freedom" Committee headed by attorney George Cosson. It demanded answers to 14 questions such as "Why have you never said a critical word about Hitler or Naziism? If Hitler is not a threat, what are we preparing for? Do you realize that to keep war out of America, our organized defense must be beyond our shore?" Lindbergh didn't get the questions before the speech and thus didn't take them up. He probably wouldn't have anyway.

Des Moines members of the American Legion appeared for the most part to be anti-Lindbergh. The Argonne Post band had been scheduled to play at the Coliseum but canceled. Robert Colflesh, prominent Des Moines attorney and a Purple Heart veteran of World War I, called Lindbergh a "topnotch saboteur of patriotism." Colflesh lost a leg at the World War I battle of Château Thierry in France, where he was wounded in five places and gassed as well.

Once Pearl Harbor happened and the United States was in war, Charles Lindbergh abruptly changed course. He dropped all neutrality efforts. The "America First Committee" dissolved.

Lindbergh had been a colonel in the Air Force reserve. He resigned the commission in 1938 after undergoing criticism from the president. Lindbergh tried to get into the service after the declaration of war but could not recover the commission.

He thereupon went into civilian military employment in a big way and made a notable contribution to the war effort anyway. As an adviser to the United Aircraft Corporation, which produced planes for battle, Lindbergh flew 50 combat missions against the Japanese in the Pacific. Those who saw him in action had only admiration for his flying ability and dedication.

President Eisenhower restored Lindbergh to the military in 1954 and promoted him to brigadier general in the reserve. All doubts as to his innate patriotism had long since gone away.

Hanford MacNider likewise wanted very much to return to the service once the war was on, and he succeeded in regaining a commission in the army. He had a brilliant career as a combat officer in the South Pacific, where he was wounded in action. He emerged from the war as a brigadier general.

Despite all his work in trying to keep the United States neutral in the pre–World War II period, one of his Iowa colleagues acclaimed MacNider as the finest citizen-soldier in the state's history.

Armistice Wrath

A t least 125,000 turkeys froze to death in northwest Iowa alone. Upwards of half the apple trees in the state were killed.

Five duck hunters died in the Mississippi River. Dozens of others barely escaped with their lives. Three army flyers were lost when their plane crashed into Spirit Lake.

Thousands of cattle and sheep were scattered all over the landscape. Some were found dead standing up. So many pheasants were killed in northwest counties that state authorities asked Iowans not to hunt the birds north of Highway 18 and west of Forest City.

That was only part of what happened when a wicked Armistice Day blizzard hit Iowa November 11, 1940. It was perhaps the most punishing storm in the state's history.

The blizzard wreaked so much havoc because it struck

sudden, devastating blows.

The preceding weather had been unseasonably warm. Fruit trees thought it was spring again. Buds started to swell, sap to rise in the trunks. Frost-sensitive tomato plants were still green in early November.

The turnaround was unbelievably swift. The temperature before dawn at 5:30 that morning was a balmy 54 in Des Moines. A howling west wind sprang up. By 6:30, the thermometer had plummeted to 32, a drop of 22 degrees in one hour. The wind chill was already one below zero. By 7:30, the mercury was down to an icy 23. The wind increased to 32 and then to a destructive 50 miles an hour. By 11 o'clock the temperature was 18 and the wind chill close to 30 below.

Here was the weatherman's explanation of what had happened: A lot of icy polar air accumulated in Canada just north of the border. At the same time, a "low" gathered force in Colorado, then traveled eastward to Oklahoma, took a left turn and surged almost due north into the Midwest. The low pulled the icy Canadian air down into Iowa and other midwestern states. The warm air in the low was full of moisture. The result was huge amounts of devastating, blowing snow. Primghar in northwest Iowa got the most, 17 quick inches, Cushing 13 inches, Estherville and Sanborn 12 inches each.

Iowans, who had been basking in the preceding enjoyable weather, were caught unprepared. Car radiators froze by the thousands. Drifts six to eight feet high blocked roads and streets.

Exhausted from flying desperately ahead of the storm, ducks dropped in large numbers almost into the laps of hunters all up and down the Mississippi River. Never before had hunters enjoyed such phenomenal shooting.

But the scene changed with violent abruptness. Now it no longer was a question of hunters bagging ducks but of saving their own lives. The gale churned up huge waves in the river, overturned boats, washed away blinds. Leonard Reynolds of Muscatine drowned when his boat capsized near Burlington. Arveila Young of Fort Madison was found drowned under his boat. Three hunters froze to death in a blind.

Norman Childers of Dallas City, Illinois, had come to the Iowa side of the river to hunt. He told his harrowing story afterwards from a Fort Madison hospital bed.

> Right after I got out on the river all hell broke loose, raining and blowing like nothing I had seen in my life before. The waves piled up as high as this room and it was all I could do to climb up on top of one wave, ride it until it broke, then climb up on another before the boat was swamped. I didn't dare let go of the oars long enough to put on my heavy coat, and I was soaked in a few seconds.

The driving rain turned to snow. Childers estimated that the wind shot up to 60 miles an hour. Luckily, he got into an empty and intact blind.

> I had a hole in my boot and I could feel the cold creeping up. Every once in a while during the night I would get drowsy and the pain of the cold seemed to melt away. But I knew I was lost if I let that go on, so I would sit up in the boat and unbutton my coat so the wind would whip me awake again.
>
> I yelled and sang and blew on my duck squawker to help keep awake. Any sound was better than just the waves pounding all the time, and the wind.
>
> I kept pounding my left foot and trying to move around as much as I could to keep the circulation going but I was all covered with ice clear to my skin and could hardly move.

What saved Childers was the arrival of a naval launch.

"When the navy men threw me a line," he said, "I could hardly get my hands off the oars because they were frozen on, but I was so glad I cried."

The loss of eight lives in Iowa was small compared with the toll in other midwestern states. Seventy-three died in Michigan, 49 in Minnesota and 23 in Wisconsin.

Elsewhere in Iowa, the merciless blizzard drove cattle through fences and forced them southeast as far as 10 miles from home pastures. Niels Nielsen, an Alta farmer, found some of his cattle the next day on the streets of Storm Lake, more than six miles away. Fifteen cattle barged into Aurelia, then stampeded east out of town and were gathered up in Alta, seven miles away.

Kenneth Tifft, Sanborn farmer, said 16 head of his cattle froze to death and three others were crippled. An O'Brien County farmer lost 14 hogs when snow filled his hoghouse. Wallace Scott found 100 dead lambs frozen to the ground. Chickens were found hanging dead from their roosts at Le Mars. At Cherokee, Ray

Frances saved only 63 of his 2,500 turkeys, and at Kingsley, C.W. Spaan lost 2,700 turkeys. Walter Wesalink at Sheldon, dug 700 of his 1,700 turkeys out from under the snow.

The kill of apple trees was tremendous all over the state. The counties where apples were grown commercially in 1940 included Harrison, Polk, Fremont, Mills, Page, Pottawattamie, Madison, Des Moines, Henry, Lee, Louisa and Van Buren. These counties produced 485,000 bushels of apples in 1940. The next year their production sank to a mere 74,000 bushels. The apple industry didn't fully recover for many years.

The storm tore roofs off downtown office buildings in Davenport and the wreckage blocked two downtown streets. At Moulton the raging wind blew down a brick schoolhouse wall. (No pupils were present.) Sixty-five stranded travelers crammed one farmhouse south of Storm Lake. They ate a bushel of popcorn, lots of apples and other food, and sat up all night reciting poetry and telling stories. Eighty others were marooned in a Sioux Valley dance pavilion. They didn't have much to eat but the supply of beer was plentiful.

The Eldora Riot

A dozen boys overturned a table with a crash, spilling food and dishes in every direction.

The upset table was the signal for swarms of youths to throw dishes against the walls, to kick out doors and windows and to dash for freedom.

It was a full-blown riot at the state training school for boys at Eldora. Officials stood by, all but helpless as 179 boys smashed the dining room and staged a mass escape August 29, 1945.

Brutal treatment of kids touched off the revolt. Young inmates had been beaten repeatedly with blackjacks and clubs for disciplinary reasons. Some were placed in cells and left fastened with their arms manacled outside the bars.

Worst of all, Ronald L. Miller, 17, of Des Moines, died of a skull injury the day before the mutiny. He had been hit in the head with a blackjack by a school official and then had been forced to work for six hours on a coal pile in a hot sun. He collapsed and expired in the hospital.

The escapees scattered all over the north central counties of the state. Another 46 boys ran away in the next few weeks. It took some time to round up the runaways and restore control of the overcrowded institution and its 580 problem youths.

The Eldora school was established in 1886 to straighten out delinquent and incorrigible boys. Iowa courts have committed boys to Eldora for more than a century for holdups, thefts, vandalism, inflicting injuries and other criminal acts.

The danger of over-discipline was recognized from the beginning. Said one of the early trustees: "By too much severity, the moral object of penal establishments is thus in fact defeated, which should be not so much to punish as to reform—to receive boys idle and ill-intentioned and return them to society if possible as honest and industrious citizens."

The riot shocked the people of Iowa. Governor Robert Blue removed O.S. Von Krog as superintendent of the school. Blue said "unjustifiably severe discipline measures" had been used.

Investigation disclosed the school had been poorly operated as well as being beyond capacity. The staff was too small and far from expert. The employees maintained control all too often through cruelty and fear. Classroom work in the academic school was called inadequate. Living in each of the cottages were two and a half times as many boys as could be properly supervised, reports said.

Von Krog, a longtime schoolman, found himself in major trouble. He and other staffers were indicted on charges of conspiring to beat up seven inmates. Von Krog was guilty of no such conspiracy and the charges against him were dropped.

Von Krog said with considerable truth that he had never received anywhere near enough money from the Legislature to do a good job of running the place. He denied any knowledge of extreme cruelty although he did say: "I believe paddling under supervision is the only sort of discipline some boys understand."

State officials agreed privately that perhaps Von Krog did not know all that was going on. The officials, however, said Von Krog should have known, that he did not keep good track of what the staff was doing.

The governor sent Iowa State Guard troops to Eldora to

secure the situation. Warden Percy A. Lainson of Fort Madison penitentiary took over as temporary superintendent.

The grand jury also indicted two former guards, Carl Klatt and Harold Nelson, for second degree murder in the death of Ronald Miller. The indictments charged that "cruelty, brutality and bestiality" were all too prevalent at the school. The jury added: "We are convinced beyond any doubt that for both minor and serious infractions of the rules, boys have been beaten with blackjacks, wooden billy clubs and other instruments of brutality. Greater emphasis has been placed on the raising of good hogs and cattle than on the rehabilitation of boys." (Eldora, like all institutions of the time, also operated adjacent state-owned farms.)

The story was not all one-sided, of course. The youths were there because of misdeeds back home, some of them major. In 1945, the year before the riot, a training school official commented:

> We have boys who probably should be in Anamosa Reformatory. With quarters crowded, they sometimes put wrong ideas into other boys' heads. We don't have facilities to segregate some of these repeaters who have come here a second and third time. The discipline problem could be reduced 75 percent if the cottages were not so crowded.

Lainson shook up the school staff soon after taking over. He fired 20 employees in a sweeping reorganization.

Loss of jobs proved to be the principal punishment meted out. Juries did not convict Klatt and Nelson of murder but only of assault. Each was committed to 30 days in jail.

The Miller youth was sent to Eldora the first time in 1943 when he was 15. He was released and got into the army when he lied about how old he was. He had advanced to corporal when officers found out he was underage and discharged him. About two months before his death, he was returned to Eldora for parole violation and intoxication.

The story of Miller's last hours of life is grim. School authorities heard that a group of seven boys headed by Miller was planning to escape. The boys were brought to the basement of the disciplinary cottage about midnight August 27.

What followed resembled a one-sided free-for-all fight, according to the boy-witnesses.

Miller got the first "licking," and what a horrible thing it was.

A witness who had just arrived in the cottage testified at the inquest that Miller's head was already bleeding when he tried unsuccessfully to hit Klatt with a chair. Klatt responded by striking Miller with a "leather tug" and knocked him down.

Klatt, the witness added, invited Miller to get up and take his beating. Miller at first was unable to rise and said, "I can't see."

Miller next was taken to the "whipping post" where Nelson struck him 17 times, presumably with a "tug" or club. The witnessing boys were required to count the blows out loud. As the 17th landed, Miller cried out, "I can't stand any more!" Whereupon Nelson sat on Miller as Klatt broke a blackjack beating him on the head, witnesses said.

Miller broke away, ran into the restroom, grabbed a chair and broke it on Klatt. The guard retaliated by requiring other boys to hold Miller as he struck the youth 30 more times.

Another of the boys testified that the "rest of us got ours" (beatings) after the guard let up on Miller. Every boy suspected of plotting the break was clipped on the head with a blackjack by Nelson as he left.

But the ordeal didn't end there. Miller and his friends were taken to a bedroom upstairs and required to stand by their beds, apparently a couple of hours, until 3 o'clock in the morning.

Miller was sick and "threw up his breakfast" before being forced to start shoveling coal at 7 o'clock in the morning. He and the other six apparently were required to carry large shovels of coal about 50 feet, from one pile to another for no good reason, "just to have something for the boys to do." They had to do it "on the double" for one hour, then could walk for half an hour. They could stop for a drink of water now and then.

A witness said he saw several boys drop from exhaustion, including Miller. One boy said he helped carry Miller to the hospital when it became obvious that he was far gone. Miller died at 2 o'clock the next morning.

After calm was established under Lainson at the school, the state appointed Fred Cooper as permanent superintendent. Cooper had been a highly regarded athletic coach and high school official at Fort Dodge for 22 years.

Cooper halted all physical punishment at Eldora, recruited a psychiatrist to work with mentally troubled youths, transferred retarded boys to other institutions and arranged for the temporary shift of some 90 hopelessly bad boys to Anamosa Reformatory.

Cooper worked so hard at his new job that he may have shortened his own life. His weight dropped from 192 pounds to 178 pounds in three months. In less than two years he was dead at age 51.

Cooper had to combat deep suspicion among the Eldora boys. Some youngsters refused to take medicine during a flu epidemic.

"They acted like we were trying to poison them," he said. "It took us several months to get them all well again."

Coming from a high school of mostly normal youngsters, Cooper was disgusted at the perversion he found at Eldora. "I never realized what boys could and would do," he said.

He did his best to keep their spare time occupied in athletics. "The busier we keep them in sports, the better off they will be," he commented. "We want to tire them out playing."

Von Krog is a tragic figure in the history of the school. He was not permanently shunned, however. In 1946, at 67 years of age, he was made an honorary life member of the Iowa State Education Association.

Von Krog once said, "There is no such thing as a bad boy. Subject them to training and discipline and they are just about certain to come out all right."

He asserted that parents were responsible for 60 percent of the problems of training school boys. "Improper home life and poor home training are by far the most frequent reasons for boys being sent to us," he said. "It's a shame that it's the boy who is penalized. The parents are the ones who should be punished."

Von Krog constantly protested to legislators regarding the insufficiency of the funds he received to operate the school. The amount spent for salaries and maintenance of 86 school employees was $88,809, not much more than $1,000 per worker per year, low even for these Depression times. Von Krog's salary certainly was not munificent. He drew only $3,000 a year. But he did receive maintenance, that is, food and living quarters.

Talk to Jesus

F ourteen eighth graders bowed their heads and said the Lord's prayer at the end of a lesson in a public school room at Roland, Iowa. The textbook they used had nothing to do with such school subjects as mathematics and science. The book was titled *An Explanation of the Catechism.*

In the same room later in the day, a third grade class studied the Bible. On the blackboard appeared such sentences as "It is more blessed to give than to receive. Services tonight at 7:30. Salem church."

A Minneapolis evangelist came to another class to answer questions. In response to one wide-eyed boy's query, the evangelist said yes, we will all get to talk to Jesus personally, and to other Biblical characters, too, after Judgment Day.

Back in 1948, Roland was one of several Iowa districts teaching religion in public schools. Some districts, however, didn't hold the classes in school buildings but released the pupils to attend churches for instruction during school hours. Charles City used that method. Other districts reportedly with religious education programs included Randall, Bode and St. Lucas.

A 1948 decision by the U.S. Supreme Court on the religious education question aroused considerable anxiety in Lutheran Roland, a Norwegian-American town of 800 in Story County. The high court said a school board in Illinois had to cease religious instruction on school days in school buildings because it was contrary to the constitutional principle of separation of church and state. Which was exactly what Roland had been doing for decades.

One of the 15 classrooms in the red-brick Roland school was used solely for religious education. All 197 children in the first eight grades spent up to 30 minutes each school day in that room.

One teacher, Margaret Holthe, spent full time on religion. She was not on the district payroll, however. Her salary and other expenses of the program were met in large part by contributions of 20 cents a week from parents of each child. The fund also received donations from church members who had no children. Cost of the entire program, including the Holthe salary, was about $1,500 a year. (Pay and other costs were far lower in 1948 than in the 1990s.)

There was nothing new in all this. Roland set up the religious department in the school 31 years earlier, in 1917. The townspeople decided to establish such a department rather than start a Lutheran parochial school. Such a school in the 95 percent Lutheran community would have wrecked the public school.

Roland people agreed in 1948 that continuing religious instruction in the school would have been most difficult if anybody objected. But that was only a remote possibility because the community was so solidly Lutheran and Norwegian-American. The two Evangelical Lutheran churches in town reportedly had a combined membership of 1,800, or more than twice Roland's population. The number of farm families belonging to the town churches obviously was considerable.

One Catholic dad, Ray Breen, had a second grade daughter who took Lutheran religion in the school along with the rest of the kids. Breen worked in the lumberyard. He described himself as "the only Irishman around here."

"I am 100 percent in favor of religious instruction in public schools so long as it doesn't become catechitical [preaching]," Breen said. "Attendance isn't compulsory anyway." He took his daughter to the nearby town of Nevada every Saturday for Catholic instruction.

Roland leaders credited the religious instruction with giving the community a higher type of young people, and adults as well.

"The kids get a lot of good out of this program," said C.P. Thompson, the school superintendent. "They get a background that stays with them the rest of their lives. Our youngsters are pretty well behaved, due to their church training, home environment and this religious department.

"When you see basketball players going home with Bibles under their arms, it makes an impression on you."

The Reverend Olaf Holen of the Salem church said discontinuing the program would have been "almost catastrophic." He asserted that Roland people were good church people in part because of the religious education they got in their school days.

The Reverend Allen E. Nelson of the Bergen church said the juvenile problem was less acute in Roland than elsewhere because of the religious training.

This department has done a magnificent job of building up the

moral tone of the community. I have noticed the difference in
boys and girls coming out of this school and those I have met
in other parishes I have held.

We haven't any of our youth in the toils of the law that
I know of.

Though the program was described as voluntary, no child
refused to enroll in 1948, or perhaps ever up to that time. No
school credit was given for the course but Miss Holthe did give
grades. She took over as religion teacher in 1943. She was a
graduate of the Lutheran Bible Institute in Minneapolis.

No rent was paid for the religion room with its 25 seats. First
sponsors wanted to pay rent but the school board decided that
would be a case of taking money out of one pocket and putting it
in another. Pretty much the same people would have been involved
in both the paying (taxes) and receiving (rent).

The school had a six-hour day. It started at 9 a.m. and was
out at 3:40 p.m., with 40 minutes for lunch. Thompson said the
time for religious instruction was obtained by cutting off a few
minutes of other classes here and there. He maintained that if any
real time was lost in regular school instruction it didn't show up in
the caliber of the pupils. Roland children were well above the
average for the state in the "every pupil" test given by the
University of Iowa, he said.

The Roland school was considered one of the good ones in
the state in its population class, Thompson reported, and met the
requirements of the state courses of study. The superintendent said
the children learned English and some grammar and did memory
work in the religion classes, all helpful in the learning process.

Every Friday the children brought offerings for missionary
work around the world. Each grade had a mission to which they
contributed. First grade money, for example, went to Alaska, and
the amount was $7.67 for the first two and a half months of 1948.
The total received from all classes in that period was $83.20.

There was nothing halfway about the religion that was taught
in the Roland public building.

"We should have a militant church, a fighting church," Miss
Holthe told the eighth grade class. "Does that mean fighting
among ourselves? No, it means fighting the devil, the world and
our flesh."

The class held a discussion on "sanctification," which was described as "spiritual cleansing." Miss Holthe took occasion to point out the importance of outward cleanliness. "The person who really professes to be a Christian has no business going around dirty and sloppy," she said.

She also was critical of the people she called "hypocrites": "A person may go to church on Sunday and live an absolutely contrary life during the week," she commented. "He may be the biggest crook ever during the week. It isn't what you are only on Sunday but every single day."

She assigned a lesson to the eighth graders in the catechism textbook. The pupils were told to study several questions and answers, of which the following was one: "What precious gift does the Holy Spirit grant you in the Christian church?"

"In the Christian church He daily forgives abundantly all my sins and the sins of all believers. Everyone that believeth in Him shall receive remission of sins (Acts 10:43)."

The introduction of the textbook said, "This revised explanation of Luther's catechism is based upon the explanations of Pontoppidan, Sverdrup, Laache, Yivisaker and Tanner. It has been prepared for instruction in confirmation classes and for pastors and teachers who prefer the question and answer method of teaching."

In other classes Miss Holthe used such texts as were provided through the Sunday school graded system compiled by the board of education of the Evangelical Lutheran Church.

Each of the eight classes closed with prayer every day. All classes except the first grade used the Lord's prayer. The little ones had a verse of their own.

Miss Holthe adjusted the biblical stories so that the different age groups could understand them. For example, Joseph of the Old Testament was "the elevator man who stored all the grain," the same as elevator operators in Roland.

The Minneapolis evangelist, The Reverend Albert L. Abrahamson, came to the seventh grade class to answer questions. They weren't all religious. One boy wondered how many languages he spoke. The answer was two, English and Norwegian.

The Reverend Mr. Abrahamson, large, wide-faced and bespectacled, covered a lot of ground in the class session.

"How does God know when we are doing wrong?" was one

question. The evangelist quoted several passages from the scriptures to prove that "wherever we go God sees us."

He also told the youngsters that the world was destroyed by floods in the time of Noah and his ark, and would be consumed by fire the next time. Anybody who pretends to be able to forecast when that will be "doesn't know what he is talking about." The same applies to the second coming of Christ, he said.

"Will all the planets be ruined when the earth is burned?" asked a black-haired lad wearing a sweatshirt.

"Who knows?" answered the clergyman. "There will be a new Heaven and a new earth. I am just as anxious to know the answer to that question as you are. There is going to be an entirely new setup."

As elsewhere, the times had changed drastically in Roland by the 1990s. The Roland school district had merged with nearby Story City. And religious instruction in the school was long gone. The program was abandoned after both parents and students had grown cold to it.

Red Faces

T he biggest upset ever in American presidential elections stunned the experts in 1948, and Iowa was right in the middle of it.

Democrat Harry Truman befuddled the pollsters and political writers that year by shellacking the favorite, Republican Tom Dewey, for the presidency.

Practically without exception the analysts had predicted easy going for Dewey. Pollster George Gallup said Dewey would win "with a substantial number of electoral votes." Elmo Roper announced he was quitting polling early. He said it was no use to continue because it was so one-sided for Dewey.

Fifty political writers were polled and every one tabbed Dewey as the winner. There were plenty of red faces coast to coast the next day.

Usually perceptive *Des Moines Register* writers Dick Wilson and William Mylander declared, "It's a Republican year. Thomas

E. Dewey will win in a walk."

Forecasts were the same for Iowa—that Dewey would carry the state hands down. After all, he had captured Iowa over the champ, President Franklin Roosevelt, by 47,000 votes in 1944. Who in his right mind would expect upstart Truman to accomplish in 1948 what Roosevelt couldn't four years earlier? The Iowa Poll conducted by the *Register* gave Dewey a one-sided 54-41 edge in the state.

Even *Register* columnist Harlan Miller got into the act. He wrote that "Tom's young for a President. He will be two months short of 47 when he's inaugurated."

They were all wrong, wrong, wrong. Fighting Harry piled up a smashing victory with 303 electoral votes to Dewey's 189. Truman won by upwards of two million popular votes. Gallup had foreseen a Dewey victory by two million.

Iowan Henry Wallace, running on a third-party Progressive ticket, got no electoral votes. Strom Thurmond, a longtime senator from South Carolina, carried four states and 38 electoral votes in the Deep South as the candidate of the Dixiecrats. Neither Wallace nor Thurmond fatally fragmented the Democratic vote as was expected.

Iowa had been pronounced safe for Dewey by up to 60,000 votes. Instead Truman won the state by 28,000. The same thing happened in such other presumed "Dewey" states as Ohio, Wisconsin, Illinois, Colorado and Wyoming.

Register cartoonist Ding Darling drew a funny cartoon the day after the 1948 election under the title: "One-Man Army." Ding pictured a smiling Truman dusting himself off, with a heap of Republicans, polls and Dixiecrats in a junk pile behind him.

But there were no smiles among pollsters and writers. Embarrassed George Gallup, a native of Jefferson, Iowa, said, "Truman captured many votes from Wallace. Also, a lot of undecideds voted for Truman." Gallup added that polling was "still an inexact science."

Shamefaced Roper, who had predicted a 52–37 runaway for Dewey, confessed, "I could not have been more wrong. The thing that bothers me the most is that I do not know why I was wrong."

Dick Wilson owned up to having missed the boat and said, "The man on the street escaped the notice of political writers and he clearly was dissatisfied."

National columnist Marquis Childs, a native of Clinton, Iowa, commented, "The fatal flaw was reliance on public opinion polls. No amount of rationalization can explain the mistakes of Gallup, Roper & Company."

The *Chicago Tribune* attained unwanted fame with the headline "Dewey Defeats Truman" but only in relatively few early edition papers. The closest the *Register* came to trouble was a headline in an early edition saying "Key States Going for Dewey." Quite a few papers didn't look very good in early editions.

The *Washington Post* invited the victorious Truman to dine with correspondents, Truman eating turkey while the newsmen ate roasted crow. It isn't known whether the dinner ever came off.

Truman and Dewey had campaigned in different ways. Combative Harry charged September 18 at Dexter, Iowa, that the Republican Congress had "stuck a pitchfork in the back of the farmer." Speaking to a rural crowd of 80,000, Truman also blasted the "gluttons of privilege" of Wall Street.

In contrast, low-key Dewey said two days earlier in Des Moines that "we enter upon a campaign to unite America." He opened his national campaign with that mild theme before 16,000 at Drake University.

Those two speeches set the pattern of the campaign: Dewey playing it cozy, thinking he was sitting on a safe lead; Truman staging an all-out battle against what appeared to be insurmountable odds. In the end the fighter won.

Truman went hot and heavy after the farm vote. Farmers were well heeled in 1948 after the prosperous World War II years. Truman reminded them of the supports the Democratic New Deal had provided since the depths of the Depression in the 1930s.

"There is every reason for the farmer to expect a long period of good prices if he continues to get a fair deal," Truman said at Dexter. "His great danger is that he may be voted out of a fair deal and into a Republican deal."

He landed another effective punch when he accused the 1947–1948 Republican Congress of refusing to vote on-the-farm storage facilities for grain.

Then, just before America went to the polls, Truman said a Democratic victory "would be the best insurance against going back to the dark days of 1932."

It so happened that the price of corn went down a bit before the 1948 vote. The price per bushel ranged from $1.25 to $1.40 early in October (not bad for the times). It then dropped to $1.20 to $1.27 the middle of the month and down to $1.14 just before the November election. That was a loss of more than a dime a bushel in a month, a significant amount then.

At the same time, the harvest of the biggest corn crop up to that time approached 3.6 billion bushels nationally, the first 3 billion bushel crop in history. Even lower corn prices loomed. Thus, it is understandable that last-minute farm voting switches took place. The farmers figured their chances of getting price protection from the Democrats were better than from the Republicans.

The narrowness of Truman victories in a number of states could be explained by farm defections from Dewey. There were many more farm voters in 1948 than in the 1990s. (The farm population was much larger.) And Truman didn't carry the swing states all that much. Besides his small edge of 28,000 in Iowa, he squeezed out a win of only 43,000 in much larger Illinois and a mere 7,000 in Ohio, under 5,000 in Wyoming, fewer than 28,000 in Colorado and 57,000 in Wisconsin.

It must be said, however, that Truman also did better

JAKE MORE

than expected in urban America, even including Iowa cities. Dewey lost the seven Iowa counties with the largest cities by 151,500. That was 25,000 worse than his showing in those countries four years earlier. If he had done as well there in 1948 as he had in 1944, he would have come close to offsetting Truman's 28,000 margin in Iowa.

Truman had pounded on such things as favoring a boost in the minimum wage from 40 cents to 75 cents an hour, slum clearance and low rent housing, and opposing labor laws hated by unions. These issues evidently boosted his urban support.

The elated Truman managers said the day after election that "it all started in Iowa." They credited Iowa Democratic Chairman Jake More with organizing large crowds for Truman at Dexter and at whistle stops in his first midwestern swing.

More also received the president's undying gratitude by insisting that Truman would carry Iowa, no matter what the polls and writers said.

The pugnacious Truman evidently came to believe in his heart that he would triumph. He said right before the polls opened, "The people are with us. The tide is rolling. All over the country I have seen it in the people's faces."

The Associated Press called Truman the best pollster of them all.

Teen-age Tragedy

E ighteen-year-old Francis Elwood plowed all day on the farm where he worked, near Hampton, Iowa. After a supper of wieners, he went up to his room to write some letters. He was tired. He planned to go to bed early.

He didn't know that he had a date with death in three hours.

In Hampton, George Kibsgaard also didn't know that he had only three hours to live.

George, 18, had helped his electrician father move a meter in a house that day. After supper, George took his aged Oldsmobile and went uptown, just as he always had done. It was so routine that he didn't even say goodbye to his parents.

In the west part of town, Russell Jensen, 19 and young-looking for his age, washed up in the little back-lot house where he lived with his father. Russ had polished cars that day in the Ford garage. Now he was going to have a bowl of chili at the Skelly lunchroom where the teen-agers hung out.

Russell similarly had no realization of the fact that the end of his life was only hours away.

Lloyd Casey, 18, a likable redhead, went home from the *Hampton Chronicle* where he was working as a printer-apprentice.

He also thought he would drop over to the Skelly lunchroom after the evening meal.

The march of events was to claim Lloyd's life too, very soon.

In two other homes, boys ate at the family tables, perhaps looked at comic books, talked on the telephone, got ready to go out for a while.

As the minutes ticked away that Tuesday night in November 1949, the cast slowly gathered for the tragedy in which four were to die. The question came up, shall there be any girls in on this? As it worked out, none were involved.

Jane Maneely, 16, had been along at other times when George and Lawrence "Sleepy" Muhlenbruck laughingly darted out of the grasp of death. She was not to be on hand this time, however. She had a job for the evening taking care of children. She needed the money.

Also, Bonnie Jones and Bonnie Martin might have been in the cast. They chose to stay at the Dixie Inn instead of riding with the boys.

In the Skelly lunchroom, meanwhile, a dozen youths had gathered. Russ Jensen had his bowl of chili. He kidded Elsie Woodley, the waitress, telling her it was only hot tomato sauce.

The jar with $1 bills and half-dollars, "in Remembrance of the Boys," wasn't out yet. That was to come later.

Carl Jensen, father of Russell, was in the lunchroom, too, having a cup of coffee.

Russell Bonjour, 22, played the pinball machine, as several boys clustered around. Jensen had a bottle of pop. Somebody broke a salt shaker.

Elsie didn't like the loss of the shaker. To punish the boys, the waitress pulled the plug on the pinball machine so that nobody could play.

The fellows all sat quietly on the stools for a minute, "just to show me they knew how to act," said Elsie.

In the crowd was Muhlenbruck, 18, who had done considerable chasing around in cars. He had his 1936 Ford parked outside. Parked there also was George Kibsgaard's 1936 Olds. Kibsgaard was perhaps an even bigger highway menace than "Sleepy," but neither of them, or any of the other boys for that matter, indulged in liquor.

George, though, had been fined twice in the last six months

for reckless driving. "Sleepy" was in court in 1948 at the same time as George. The two youths several nights before had been in a near crash with each other out on the highway. At least once before they may have scraped front fenders.

At least one of them also thought there was something manly about roaring down the highway at night without headlights. Their idea of a good time was to play "swerve" with cars going 60 to 70 miles an hour.

Waitress Elsie remembered later that on the fateful night Kibsgaard and Francis Elwood were not in the lunchroom but "out in front."

It was getting toward 8 o'clock, time to go.

Russ Bonjour, oldest of the bunch, brought along some apples and gum.

For the next half hour, where the boys went and what they did, nobody seemed to know.

But this is known: About 8:30 the two automobiles dashed along Highway 3 west of Hampton. Kibsgaard, going west, had the Olds wide open at 73. Speeding east was "Sleepy's" car. Kibsgaard had two passengers and himself. Muhlenbruck had four and himself.

At least one car had the lights off.

Death waited in the pleasant moonlight night, just east of a stone farmhouse, 6½ miles west of town.

The highway patrol said one car was 18 inches over the middle of the road, the other 14. That was the story the marks told on the concrete. Unless somebody swerved, a collision was inevitable.

With a tearing impact of metal on metal and flash, the two cars met in a terrific crash. Whether the drivers didn't see each other or were testing each other's nerve is uncertain.

Kibsgaard's bluish-green Olds literally climbed up on the left side of the Muhlenbruck car. The Olds flew through the air. Bodies hurtled from the seats. The car landed with a crunch on the shoulder, with its rear wheels down in the ditch.

It also landed on top of Francis Elwood, the boy who was going to write some letters that night and go to bed early. The muffler pressed down on Elwood's face, broke his nose, smashed in his features and seared the skin. Undoubtedly unconscious, he suffocated.

They didn't even find the Elwood body until one and a half hours later when a highway patrolman happened to turn a flashlight on the bottom of the car and he saw a shoe sticking out.

Kibsgaard died quickly, perhaps immediately. His face and head were crushed beyond recognition.

Jensen lived until 7 o'clock the next morning. He had a fractured skull and a scalp wound that bled interminably. His face was swollen, he was cut from flying glass, he was cold and clammy with shock.

Lloyd Casey, 18, had a badly cut throat, cuts on his face, abdominal injuries, a left leg in which the bones were shattered. He died three nights later.

"Sleepy" Muhlenbruck had four fractures in the pelvis, a broken left arm, a right shoulder blade fracture and severe cuts and abrasions. He couldn't drive a car for months even if the authorities had let him.

Bonjour had a broken left arm and leg, severe facial cuts and bruises and a sprained left shoulder. Leon Casey, 16, Lloyd's brother, had a tear in the flesh of his face from the corner of one lip back toward the ear. He lost all his upper and lower teeth, suffered a crushed nose and a broken right wrist.

Merlin Numelin, 16, suffered a possible skull fracture. The left side of his head was badly swollen.

M.J. Greenfield, a Hampton undertaker, said afterward, "If all the teen-agers in town could have been out there picking up those boys, it would have been the best lesson in driving they ever could have."

Wilbur Kenison, a 17-year-old high schooler, did go through that experience.

Patrolman Davis asked me to help him. We took Muhlenbruck on a stretcher to the ambulance. He was conscious. His eyes were open. His left leg was broken and there was a big hole in his chest. I figure the post of the steering wheel punched the hole in his chest. He was saying "oh, my leg." His shirt was ripped open and I could see the hole. Most of the blood seemed to be coming out of the chest.

We brought Russ Jensen in too. We laid him on the floor of the ambulance. When the ambulance hit the railroad tracks going to town, his legs uncrossed and he gave a little moan. I held Muhlenbruck up. He wanted to keep rolling over on his stomach. Jensen's head was between my feet, sort of.

When I got to the hospital, the nurses said I looked white as a sheet. I felt like one too.

The toll of four dead and four injured shook Hampton, a town of 4,400, to its foundations. It also uncovered some startling things about teen-age driving in the north Iowa area.

The condition wasn't peculiar to north Iowa, however. The teen-age traffic death rate for Iowa in 1949 was four or five times worse than that of the adult driver.

Jane Manelly, whose life may have been saved because she had to take care of children that night, said some amazing things in an interview. Jane often had gone riding with Kibsgaard and Elwood. She wore Elwood's motorcycle ring attached to a chain around her neck.

"I like reckless driving and I like speed," she said frankly. "It's only something like this that teaches you a lesson when somebody awfully close to you is killed. I don't think you can learn, only by experience.

" I was in a motorcycle accident once but that didn't bother me." (She had a couple of stitches in her head and a scar on her

THE REMAINS of Lawrence Muhlenbruck's 1936 Ford
Courtesy of the Des Moines Register

leg.) "But this accident has jarred me quite a bit."

Jane wasn't sure, however, but that "this spell" would wear off and she would crave speed again. She said she had ridden on a motorcycle going 105 miles an hour. Her top speed in a car also was 105. An adult was driving that car, incidentally.

"Just cruising along at 55 or 60 on a motorcycle satisfies me perfectly," she related. "When it gets up to 75 or 80 I get a little wary."

She didn't believe it would do any good to bar young drivers from the highways. Probably just as many would be driving without drivers licenses as there are now.

Jane gave an insight into how Hampton teen-agers of the times tore around in cars. "We would be cruising around in George Kibsgaard's car," she said. "Pretty soon 'Sleepy' Muhlenbruck would start following us. We never followed him, he always followed us. We would go out on the highway and outdistance him, then double back on a gravel road. George's car was faster than Sleepy's."

"The day George got his carburetor fixed," she recalled, "we went out to see how fast it would go. Seventy-five was the top. It got up to 80 once but came right back down. . . . It's just a matter of luck that I wasn't along the night of the crash. If I hadn't been baby-sitting, I would have."

In describing other teen-age driving escapades, Jane told of the practices of "rat racing" and "swerve." She said rat racing consisted of one car racing to pass another. "In swerving, you just swerve the car down the road, back and forth, back and forth, just enough to give it a gentle rock," she said.

Jane was along on two close calls. Once teen-agers "nearly hit" another car and another time they almost went into the ditch. Still another time she was out "bushwhacking" with George. (Bushwhacking was the practice of turning a spotlight on a parked couple.)

Jane told of another occasion in which Kibsgaard and an unnamed youth tried to see who had the most nerve. Two cars came at each other. The "bravest" would be the driver who would refuse to turn out to avoid a head on crash. "The other fellow never did pull out," Jane said. "George pulled out and didn't touch the other car."

She expressed belief that a reckless driver figures an accident always will happen to the other fellow.

"I will have to get killed on a motorcycle before I take heed of them," she observed, then added: "I just wish it were good-for-nothing kids instead of good kids who get killed."

Jane's description of Hampton teen-age driving was corroborated by signed statements by two of the boys in the hospital.

Muhlenbruck signed a statement saying he and some other boys had a highway brush with Kibsgaard several nights before. The statement said the Kibsgaard car approached with no lights on. "George whipped his car toward mine and then swerved away from us," Muhlenbruck added. "I had to pull up over the shoulder to keep him from hitting me."

Muhlenbruck said he and Kibsgaard had gone "ditching" before. "Ditching," he explained, "is where one car starts out and then tries to ditch the cars that are chasing him. It is like hide-and-seek, only it is played with cars."

He denied that the boys were playing "chicken" when the crash occurred. In chicken, two cars sped toward each other. The driver who swerved to avoid a head on collision was "chicken."

Muhlenbruck said he didn't see any vehicles coming before the crash or even any glare from lights of automobiles. "The next time I remember," he said, "was when I was talking to Patrolman Davis, who removed me from my wrecked car."

Merlin Numelin's statement told of being out riding in Muhlenbruck's car four miles south of town some time before. "George Kibsgaard came at us with no lights on and going at a pretty good clip, and Muhlenbruck had to turn so George would not hit him," Numelin said. "George had to swerve too."

Bonjour signed another statement saying he was out joyriding in Muhlenbruck's car on Highway 65 four or five nights before the accident. "George Kibsgaard was coming north in his car with his lights out and met us four miles south of town," Bonjour said. "There was a damn lot of ducking and dodging and George just barely missed us. That green Olds was an awfully big car."

Another girl acquaintance, Bonnie Jones, 18, had the idea that "these boys don't care what might happen to them. "Bonnie remembered that Kibsgaard often bragged to the girls, "Guess I'll go out and pile up the Olds."

Bonnie Jones and her friend Bonnie Martin might well have

been in the fatal crash. Kibsgaard and Leon Casey had picked up
the two girls early in the evening at the Dixie Inn. The four went to
the Heilskov farm to get Elwood. Francis was in his room getting
ready to go to bed. He decided to go to town with them instead. He
changed to his sweater and his good pants. The five then drove to
the Dixie Inn.

"The boys wanted us to go riding with them," Bonnie Jones
said, "but Bonnie Martin wanted to sit in the Dixie Inn and talk to
a boyfriend. I didn't want to be the only girl out riding. That's why
I didn't go. We promised to meet the boys afterwards."

ELSIE WOODLEY's diner in Hampton
Courtesy of the Des Moines Register

There was no afterwards.

Joe Liebendorfer handled many traffic cases in his Hampton
mayor's court. He had come to know George Kibsgaard and some
of the other youths. The mayor said Kibsgaard complained the
authorities were "picking on him."

"The last time I made the mistake of taking George's promise
and his father's promise that he would start from the ground in
learning how to drive," Liebendorfer recalled. "My first thought
was to have George's license suspended. That's what I should have
done."

The mayor expressed belief there should have been some type
of special examination given to youths applying for licenses.

"Kids who drive like that are morons in a way," the mayor

commented. "They are a minority but they are a hazard that is tremendous. They have a wanton disregard of the consequences. There should be an examination that would screen out kids of that turn of mind."

Hampton had numerous other teen-agers at the time who were in trouble with the law over driving. But those youths placed part of the blame on the adults who ran the town. One youth said, "We ain't got nothing to do in this town. All there is to do is run around in cars and chase each other. We can't even play a good game of pool without getting kicked out. Why don't they start a recreation center for us?"

Wait a Minute . . .

Sergeant John Rice was killed in action in 1950 in the Korean War. The body was sent back to the United States in 1951 for burial in Sioux City, Iowa. Graveside services were held in Memorial Park Cemetery in Sioux City. After a salute was fired and taps sounded, the Rice family and other mourners left. Workmen prepared to lower the casket into the grave.

But wait a minute. . . . Cemetery officials approached. They had noticed a number of Indians at the services. The officials asked, "Was the deceased an Indian?"

"Yes," the undertaker replied, "a Winnebago from nearby northeast Nebraska."

"Then he can't be buried here. This is for Caucasians [whites] only."

Having no choice, the undertaker took the body back to the funeral home. Workmen filled the grave. The family was notified.

The news spread swiftly across the nation.

President Truman reacted angrily in Washington. "National appreciation of patriotic services should not be limited by race, color or creed," the president declared in a telegram to acting mayor Dan Conley of Sioux City.

Truman invited Mrs. Rice to have the burial take place in Arlington National Cemetery near Washington. She accepted. Sergeant Rice was buried with full military honors in Arlington.

He lies 100 yards from the grave of John Pershing, General of the Armies in World War I.

The uproar around the country led the cemetery officials in Sioux City to recant in a hurry. They refunded the $100 Evelyn Rice had paid for the lot. They offered to allow the burial on any lot Mrs. Rice wanted, free of charge. But she had approved the Arlington arrangement.

Sergeant Rice, 37, was not a full Winnebago, and there was dispute about his family background. One report said he was 11/16 Indian and 5/16 white. A cousin said John was 3/8ths Indian and 5/8ths white. In any event, he was a great-great-grandson of Henry Rice, a U.S. senator from Minnesota in the Civil War era.

The sergeant had been in the army nine years. He enlisted right after the Japanese attack on Pearl Harbor in 1941. He was wounded in the back by shrapnel during 44 months of service in the South Pacific in World War II. The end came September 6, 1950, at Tabu-Dong in Korea.

Besides his white widow, the sergeant left three small children, the oldest 5.

The burial problem centered around the contract for the lot, which was located in an area set aside for military graves. The contract said only whites were eligible for burial there. Evelyn Rice said she didn't notice that clause when she signed the contract and she wouldn't have paid any attention to it if she had. A cemetery official tried to get her to sign an affidavit saying her husband was Caucasian. She refused.

Mrs. Rice, 29, a tall, quiet brunette, commented, "When these men are in the army, they are all equal and the same. I certainly thought they would be the same after death, especially in a military section of the cemetery."

"It was such a blow," she added, "to have this come up after we had gotten home and thought it was all over. This had been hanging over us for about a year. We buried my grandma only about a week ago."

A Sioux City delegation headed by the acting mayor called on Mrs. Rice and said city officials were "deeply shocked by this affront to our servicemen." Sioux City teachers passed a resolution condemning the "racial bigotry."

Other cemetery lot owners reacted with anger. Mrs. Fred Hadley advertised her lot for sale "as an expression of our feelings." Lot owner Ruth Rispaljo, a bank teller, said, "I thought the action was very unfair. After all, we didn't consider his race when he was fighting for his country." Wayne E. Baker, a cab operator and a veteran observed, "The Indians were in this country a long time before we were. This is an awful disgrace to the cemetery."

Memorial Park officials said all the lot contracts in the area at the time contained clauses limiting burials to white persons. The officials said their original attitude in the Rice case was prompted by fears of possible lawsuits from other lot owners insisting on white burials only.

Uncle Sam Suit

F or generations, rival Iowa candidates for public office blasted each other in campaigns. Often the speeches were, and are, harsh and vindictive.

But there were bright moments too when it was fun to observe such offbeat hopefuls as Alvin P. Meyer of Winterset in action. He was a big rawboned farmer who came out of nowhere to run for the Democratic nomination for U.S. senator in 1950. He fell far short of winning but he gave the voters plenty of chuckles.

Al ran a color picture of himself wearing a red, white and blue Uncle Sam suit in an ad he bought in the *Des Moines Sunday Register.* In the same ad he used a picture of a lot of hogs arranged in a giant letter "M" in a pasture. Meyer had spread corn in the pasture in the form of an "M." He starved the hogs for a day or so. Then, when a cameraman was ready, Meyer turned the hogs loose. They immediately formed an "M" as they rushed to the corn.

Said the ad, "Notice the letter 'M'. It denotes 'M' for Meyer for Senator."

One of his other methods of campaigning was to go into a tavern, announce who he was, and buy a beer for everybody in the place. One time an individual asked, "Boss, how about buying me a loaf of bread?" Meyer obliged. "How about a ring of baloney? Well, all right. Would you mind buying me a pound of cheese?"

"Here, I've gone as far as I can," protested Meyer. "What are you trying to pull anyway?"

"Just trying to stock up while I have the chance," the guy answered.

Al finished fourth in a six-man primary race for the senatorial nomination. He got 9,341 votes, not bad for a political unknown, and he may have polled more votes than beers he bought.

Al had plenty of money anyway. He was a successful farmer near Van Meter, Iowa. He and a brother operated 14 filling stations in six counties as well and he owned the Aldo Cafe and a grocery store in Winterset. It was said he picked up $16,000, a very sizable sum then, buying and selling corn on the Board of Trade while he was campaigning for office.

Meyer got the political bug from a lot of unexpected publicity in 1948. He wanted Harry Truman to win the presidency in the worst way that year. Al spent $85 of his own money, a tidy sum, to deliver a pro-Truman speech over radio station WHO, Des Moines. That homespun talk caught the fancy of political writers around the country. They wrote stories about Al, and how he loved the spotlight!

Even though he didn't win the nomination in 1950, Meyer did beat two other candidates. The winner was Al Loveland of Janesville, Iowa. Meyer said little that was mean about his opponents, nor did they about him. Loveland lost in the general election to Republican Senator Bourke Hickenlooper.

Meyer did win election as an Iowa State Representative later. And he came within an eyelash of capturing a Democratic nomination for Congress in 1964. Had he been the nominee, he might well have won. That was the year of the huge Governor Harold Hughes–President Lyndon Johnson Democratic landslide in Iowa. It would have been a lot of fun watching Al operate in Washington.

Al had these quaint words of wisdom about how an elected lawmaker should conduct himself over the long haul: "When your time expires, you come home honorable."

Another Iowa candidate whom the voters enjoyed was Francis Cutler of Boone. Little-known, Francis campaigned with a broom in 1932 for the Democratic nomination for lieutenant governor. "Sweep the Statehouse clean" was his motto. Of Republicans, that is. The Republicans had held the elective state offices continuously for 40 years.

To the surprise of everybody, and especially the Iowa Democratic leadership, Cutler won. He polled 52,000 votes to an opponent's 45,000 in the primary.

Party leaders didn't want to go into the general election with Francis as a nominee. They persuaded him to retire from the ticket with the promise of a good job. The Democratic state convention thereupon nominated Nelson G. Kraschel of Harlan, Iowa, for the vacancy and he was elected.

That left the leaders with the task of finding a job for Francis, and he ended up as a watchman at the Statehouse. He expected something better but was philosophical. "I am glad to have a job at the Capitol," he said. "They tell me it is warm up there in the winter and cool in the summer."

But poor Cutler lost even that position. One cloudy Sunday afternoon when the building was quiet and about empty, Francis saw a man in the gloom putting a key into the door of the state treasurer's office. Cutler fired a warning shot, probably the only shot ever fired inside the Statehouse.

The "burglar," it turned out, was State Treasurer Leo Wegman of Carroll. He had come over to do some weekend work. Wegman wasn't hit but Francis Cutler was unemployed, pronto.

Smart Mules

F armer Elmer Carlson added an extra flair to Democratic national conventions.

Like in 1952 when he took a live mule up an elevator to a fourth floor caucus of Iowa delegates in Chicago's fancy Palmer House hotel. The mule was intelligent too. It answered questions by tapping a hoof; questions that could be answered with hoof taps, that is.

In 1964 Carlson showed up with a roller-skating mule that cavorted around the convention hall at Atlantic City, New Jersey. The mule rolled in while Lyndon Johnson was waving to the cheering delegates after accepting the party's presidential nomination.

Whether all the applause was for the president was uncertain.

Onlookers felt some of the applause could have been for the mule.

Carlson, of Audubon, Iowa, said he brought the mules for the purpose of attracting "attention to the Iowa delegations in the conventions." He certainly achieved that goal.

Carlson was a delegate to both conventions and a member of the platform committee in 1964. The mules were official too, sort of. Both wore sergeant-at-arms badges.

How Elmer got Palmer House officials to allow a mule in the hotel and up an elevator was a major convention mystery in 1952. The Iowa delegation had gathered in a fourth floor suite to hear speeches by five candidates seeking the presidential nomination. They all talked. Then in came the mule, whose name, incidentally, also was Elmer.

Carlson asked the mule, "How many ballots will it take this convention to pick a nominee for president?" The animal tapped its left front foot seven times. Carlson said that meant seven ballots. (The mule was wrong. Adlai Stevenson won the nomination on the third ballot. Adlai was defeated by Republican Dwight Eisenhower for the presidency that fall.)

Palmer House officials were relieved when the mule bowed and left without committing any errors on the carpeting.

That mule belonged to Ed Pillar of Scotland, South Dakota. He brought the animal to Chicago at the request of his friend Carlson. The mule got into the convention hall too but was tethered in a corner and did not attract much attention.

In contrast, the 1964 mule stirred up controversy that even involved the White House.

Carlson thought everything had been arranged. He procured an admittance ticket and the sergeant-at-arms badge for this mule, whose name was Mickey. Elmer fastened a big button to the mule's head saying, "If I were 21, I would vote for Lyndon Johnson."

But the guards at the convention gate wouldn't let the mule in. They said they had no authority to admit such animals. The argument raged for an hour or more. There was much telephoning and conferring.

Carlson planned to have the mule come sailing in when the president was speaking. White House officials put the kibosh on that. They said Johnson planned a serious speech and they didn't want any skating mule to spoil the mood.

The opposing forces finally reached a compromise. Mickey

was to be admitted but not until the president had stopped speaking, and then only under a guard of strong men. Convention officials wanted no mule kicking delegates, TV cameramen or reporters.

The mule entered under a guard of men and nobody got kicked even a little bit.

Mickey didn't get to do as much political skating as Carlson hoped.

"Some of the delegates seated up front were plastered," Elmer said. "They wouldn't move back and make room. Mickey didn't get to show off to the fullest extent."

That mule was nine years old and belonged to a Yankton, South Dakota resident.

Carlson was a well-known Iowan prior to his mule fame. He won the world corn husking championship in 1935. He established a profitable hybrid seed corn company years before and has been credited with introducing anhydrous ammonia fertilizer in the Midwest. He owned 1,800 acres of land at his peak. He grew corn, soybeans and wheat.

But politics wasn't kind to Elmer. He ran twice for Congress, lost both times; ran for Iowa Secretary of Agriculture, got beat again.

Worse, Carlson went off the deep end when peanut farmer Jimmy Carter was elected president of the United States in 1976. Elmer's enthusiasm cost him a bundle.

"It's about time we had a farmer in the White House," declared Carlson. He thereupon went to Washington, D.C., with his head full of big plans for the January 20, 1977, inauguration.

He sincerely believed that all the farmers in the nation were as excited as he was about a farmer taking over as president. Elmer expected that farmers would pour into the capital by the tens of thousands to celebrate the inauguration. Carlson had a lot of big yellow badges made containing the words "Farmers of Iowa (or whatever state the individual was from) Welcome Carter." Carlson said, "If we're well-badged, Jimmy will know he's got some friends in town."

Elmer was not invited to the inauguration or to any of the six official parties. So he scheduled three big unofficial dances and parties for all those wandering farmers and others like himself with no place to go. He rented the ballroom of the International Inn for the nights of January 18, 19 and 20. He hired the Tommy Dorsey and Duke Ellington bands to play, as well as a Dixieland jazz band known as the Warren Covington and Clambake Seven, and the Oley Valley Hoedowners.

Elmer didn't hold back on hors d'oeuvres either, especially the clams casino, scallops and stuffed mushrooms on the last two nights (plus all kinds of good liquor at two bars). The foods the first night were the more commonplace peanuts from Georgia, popcorn from Iowa, along with hot dogs and snacks, all lubricated by the favorite beer of Billy Carter, the president's guzzling brother.

The ballroom was expensively decorated as well, "more beautiful than for an inauguration party." Elmer went first class all the way. He charged $20 to $35 admission depending on the night.

"Our purpose is to welcome Jimmy and Rosalynn to the White House and thank them for spending two years getting elected," he said. "We appreciate the work they had to do, coming from a boondocks like Plains, Georgia."

What Elmer wanted more than anything else was for Jimmy Carter or Vice President Walter Mondale to drop in at one of the parties. But Elmer found out they were fully committed elsewhere. "At least Jimmy could send his brother Billy though," he added wistfully. But Billy didn't show up either.

Carlson appeared all three nights wearing a wide-brimmed brown Stetson hat and a large bow tie. He perspired freely as he shouted greetings to newcomers and danced up a storm each night.

Carlson expected an attendance of 6,000 each night and said he had to have an average of 2,500 a night to break even.

Alas! All he got the first two nights were 200 to 250 each. The number rose to 2,000 the last night.

Elmer first estimated his loss at $250,000. He had to sell a 170-acre farm near Brayton, Iowa, for $235,000 to cover the tab. He finally said, however, that the Washington loss actually totaled about $150,000, leaving him $85,000 left over from the land sale.

His head was unbowed after the financial disaster, however. "I figured I can't take it with me," he said as he expressed hope the parties did some good. "The world is made for living. Maybe we will get people to going around and having fun instead of having long faces. It was the best week of my life."

Some Democratic leaders in Congress didn't think much of

the venture. One senator said the Iowan's lavish parties did not help the cause of getting government aid for farmers.

Iowa Senator John Culver reported that Hubert Humphrey (former vice president) said: "'Damn it, John, we were all set to get an increase in the corn loan rate, and then the members of Congress read about this Iowa farmer who has $250,000 to spend on lavish parties. We'll never get it now.'"

Whether Elmer did queer the proposed corn loan increase is not known.

Carlson has probably wished many times since that he never had put on those expensive Washington parties.

A Sight to Behold

I t was like a magnificent picture in a dream: The giant Statue of Liberty poised on a cloud of early morning fog that blotted out everything else.

That's how Kaare Mehl first saw the statue as he came into New York on ship in 1952. He was a 16-year-old immigrant bound for Iowa from his native Norway.

Mehl, who became a Story City, Iowa, building contractor, recalled, "We were all on deck staring at the fog. Suddenly we could see the outstretched arm and torch. Then the fog rolled back and there was the great figure standing alone under the wide sky, with fog covering the rest of the harbor. It was a sight to behold."

Mehl and many hundreds of other Iowans saluted the Statue of Liberty centennial in 1986 with special memories and reverence. They came long ago from foreign lands to find lifelong homes in this state.

Their first glimpse of America was the grand old lady, 300 feet high, looking out into the Atlantic from the eastern gateway to the nation. Each of these Iowans had his or her own recollection of that unforgettable moment when the statue came into view. Some expressed their memories in excellent English, others in still-accented language, but all were deeply committed to America, and to saying so.

"It was a sign of freedom. [It makes] you feel like maybe you can make it," said Louise Bliesman, 83. She arrived in Denison, Iowa, from Germany at 19 years of age in 1922.

Robert De Jager arranged to have a cabin boy awaken him and his family early on a May morning in 1951 before their ship reached New York harbor. They were en route to Pella, Iowa, from the Netherlands.

"It was a feeling of elation," said De Jager, 70. "It made a tremendous impression. I can't explain it. The title itself, the Statue of Liberty. The inscription on the base, 'Give me your tired, your poor, your huddled masses yearning to breathe free.' That explains it better than I can."

Flore Betti, 78, arrived in New York from Italy in 1933. "It was so great seeing it," she said. "It meant I have to become citizen and say what I want." She settled in Granger, Iowa.

Josie Velky, 80, of Traer, Iowa, said she was much excited: "It means freedom, so people be free." She arrived in the United States from her homeland of Czechoslovakia in 1928. She was 22.

Harry Pargas, 91, said it was a big thrill to see the big lady. He arrived in Des Moines as a 17-year-old from his native Greece in 1912. He remained an unabashed American the rest of his life. His scrapbook contained a picture of the flag with the words "God Bless America" penciled above it. Yet he originally wasn't supposed to stay. The family plan in Greece called for the teenager to travel to the United States, make as much money as possible and bring the surplus home.

"My father was killed by falling out of an olive tree," Harry said. "Times were so bad I couldn't find a job to help the family. My mother mortgaged the farm for 300 drachmas to pay me for going to America." The drachma traditionally was worth 19 cents. Thus, the mortgage appears to have been for about $57. Not much mortgage, and not much cash to pay expenses of crossing the ocean either.

A cousin arranged for young Harry to get a job shining shoes in a shine parlor located where the Equitable building is now in downtown Des Moines. Shining shoes was a booming business in those days, but has all but faded away in recent years.

"I was one of 12 shine boys," Harry said. "We were each paid $12 a month and room and board. We worked 15 hours a day weekdays and 19 hours on Saturday and early Sunday morning. That was the big day. A shine cost five cents. Farmers came in with mud on their boots up to the knee and got them cleaned for five cents. I got $10 to $15 a week in tips which I sent home."

Pargas became a partner in the business in 1920. In 1930 he opened the shoe repair department in Younkers' downtown Des Moines department store. There he stayed for 47 years until retirement. At 91 he still was dyeing shoes in his garage for old customers. He went to Greece several times but always returned.

"I did not like to stay in Greece," he said. "It was so poor, entirely different between there and here. I would not be here if I didn't like it. I work hard and make a good living. I am proud to be here."

In 1944 Harry captained the team that sold the most World War II bonds in Younkers' competition. His quota was $500; his team sold $209,000.

Louise Bliesman of Denison witnessed a rousing homecoming celebration as her ship from Germany neared New York in 1922.

"There were maybe two dozen American soldiers on board," she said. "They hadn't been home in the years after World War I which ended in 1918. When they first saw the Statue of Liberty in the distance, they went berserk. They whooped and hollered and raced around and threw their hats and ties into the Atlantic. It was noisy and wonderful."

Louise's parents had a hard time deciding where to live. They first brought her to Iowa from Germany in 1908 when she was 5 years old. The family returned to Germany in 1910 but came back to Iowa in 1912. They were on the Atlantic when the *Titanic* sank but didn't know of that great tragedy before reaching New York.

Then it was back to Germany for the Bliesmans in 1914. The reason for all the travel was the worry that the Iowa climate wasn't good for the health of Louise's mother. In 1922 Peter and Hanna Paulsen, the maternal grandparents, sent boat tickets and the Bliesman family returned to Iowa for good.

Louise sent a $10 contribution toward expenses of restoring the Statue of Liberty in 1986, its centennial year.

"It is such a thrill they are trying to keep it," she said. "Why not send a little money to help fix her up? I get a letter from a guy who instigated all this, Lee Iococca, asking another donation. Maybe I'll send them another $10. I guess they could use it."

Robert De Jager at Pella already had a family and profession before arriving in Iowa in 1951.

"I was a grade school teacher, married and had three children," he said. "A main reason that we came was that the Netherlands was so poor. Much of the nation, the harbors, had been bombed in World War II. There was a lot of unemployment. Besides, Indonesia had been set free by the Netherlands and many Dutch returned from there. The Netherlands was too crowded, with four times as many people in one-fourth the space."

De Jager and his wife were concerned about their children. "What would their future be? So we decided to go to, let's call it the land of opportunities, the land of possibilities." He said that "everything has worked out beautifully for us. We have never been sorry."

The De Jagers first went to Michigan where he taught for four years, then seven years of teaching in upstate New York, and finally to Pella where he taught in a Judeo-Christian school 16 years before retirement. He previously taught 14 years in the Netherlands.

"You also have freedom in the Netherlands but it is different," he said. "There you have a socialized, socialistic government. They wouldn't let me paint another person's house. I had to get certain papers, follow a certain course. When I came to this country and wanted to earn extra money in vacation by painting, I just did it. There was no fuss."

Italian-born Flore Betti of Granger, Iowa, knew how tough it was to be the wife of an Iowa coal miner in the Great Depression. Sometimes her husband Jerry didn't make $500 a year.

"His pay in 1933 was $5 a day and he had only 72 days of work," she said, "but he worked for farmers on other days for $1.50 a day and meals. He worked 33 years in mines at Dallas, High Bridge, Madrid No. 6 and Carney."

Even so, she said, she had "a good life in America." She returned to Italy on visits "but I am always happy to come to Iowa, my home. It was so poor in Italy."

Her husband migrated from Italy to Iowa in 1912. He went back to Italy in 1931 and met Flora, whom he married in 1932. They came to Iowa in 1933. She was 25 years old.

The Bettis were among the first in 1935 to move into one of the 50 Granger homesteads which the federal government financed and sold to low-income families. The Bettis got a brand-new two-bedroom home and three and a half acres of land for $4,000 total, which they paid off.

"I help a lot by raising strawberries," said Flora. "The strawberry money buys the groceries." The acreage produced much of the rest of the family living as well.

Josie Velky first came to Chicago from Czechoslovakia. She moved to Clutier in Tama County, Iowa, where she married a Czech carpenter. They also lived in Cedar Rapids before settling in Traer.

Josie said they found things a little better in Iowa than Chicago "but not very much pay." But she added that the United States "has been very good to me, very good." She has a sister still in Czechoslovakia who she said "is satisfied because she has to be."

Kaare Mehl got an icy reception when he arrived with his parents in Story City from Norway on Thanksgiving Day in 1952.

"The worst blizzard you ever saw was raging," he said. "I would have given anything just to stay on the train. If anybody had told me to go back home there would have been no argument. But we came out of it. The next day the sun was shining and it was all over."

Kaare's father had been in Iowa before and liked it, but his mother was hard to convince.

"They stayed in Norway 19 years after they were married before she would agree to come here," he said. Kaare's wife also was Norwegian-born.

As a boy back in Norway, Kaare had heard travelers "brag about what a great place America was." Thus, he had "high expectations."

"You know," he added, "Iowa has lived up to those brags and expectations."

He continued strong for Iowa even though his business

experienced ups and downs. He built and remodeled homes and light commercial properties.

"We feel the crunches," he commented, "but when I sit back and think about our years here and the life we've had, I don't feel that bad about it. We stick it out and we survive. No matter where you live, you'll have those kinds of times."

He regretted in 1986 that he hadn't gone to New York for the Statue of Liberty centennial celebration.

"It would have been a good reunion for us with Liberty," he said.

Spreads for Bread

Oleomargarine defeated butter in one of the angriest battles ever fought in the Iowa Legislature.

After weeks of intense struggle, the lawmakers voted in 1953 to allow food stores to sell oleo colored yellow.

The action enraged Iowa dairy farmers, whose cream was churned into butter. The farmers and their allies insisted that the yellow color belonged by nature to butter and should not be imitated in oleo, which is made from vegetable oils.

Previous state law permitted the sale of only uncolored oleo, an unappetizing white in appearance. With each package came a "bean" containing a liquid which turned the oleo yellow when kneaded into the product. It was a nuisance to have to prick the "bean" and mix the coloring into a spread for the family table.

Dairymen feared, and rightly so, that expensive butter was about to lose market share to cheaper oleo. The price of butter at the time ranged from 65 to 75 cents a pound. Oleo sold for about 32 cents a pound and that included a special state oleo tax of five cents a pound. The Legislature repealed that tax as well in the yellow oleo action. That led to a downturn in the retail oleo price to around 27 cents a pound. One grocer predicted that oleo would drop to 16 to 18 cents a pound under the new law.

The Iowa housewife wanted the cheaper price as well as yellow oleo. Nickels and dimes were more important in the family budget in the early 1950s than they are now. Butter and oleo long have competed as rival spreads for bread and toast and for use in family cooking.

The legislative conflict was a deadly serious business in 1953. Iowa was the second largest butter-producing state in the nation, 168 million pounds annually, second only to Minnesota. Iowans ate 37 million pounds of butter a year. Oleo consumption in the state totaled about 12.5 million pounds purchased legally, plus an unknown amount smuggled in.

The legislative debate got so acrimonious that one lawmaker exclaimed, "I just don't feel the quarreling should go on—everybody is getting to hate everybody else."

Arrayed against the dairy farmers in the struggle was an alliance of Iowa housewives, food store operators, oleo manufacturers and soybean farmers (whose beans were used in making oleo).

The fact that bootlegging was going on in a big way had a major impact on the legislators. Bootlegging of yellow oleo, that is. Sale of already colored oleo was legal in Missouri, Illinois, Nebraska and South Dakota, all of which border on Iowa. Travelers brought many thousands of pounds of yellow oleo from those states into Iowa. And northbound trucks from Kansas City were reputed to smuggle large quantities of yellow oleo by the case into this state. No one ever was known to have been caught and prosecuted for oleo bootlegging.

Iowa food store managers were furious over the illegal flow. There were 4,800 grocery stores in the state at the time. Particularly irked were the 2,400 managers of stores on or close to the Iowa borders. Not only were they losing oleo sales, they declared, but Iowans were buying a lot of other groceries outstate at the same time.

Senator Charles Van Eaton of Sioux City, who operated a grocery chain himself, said food stores in South Sioux City, Nebraska, were taking plenty of business away from Iowa. Van Eaton asserted Iowans were buying nearly two million pounds of yellow oleo a year in the South Sioux City stores. At the same time, he said, each Iowa customer was spending from $12 to $20 for other foods, plus additional amounts for clothing and other items they normally bought back home.

There was another factor in the situation, however. "Many people tell me they also shop outside Iowa to escape the Iowa 2 percent sales tax." Van Eaton said. Nebraska had no sales tax at the time.

Then there was bothersome Mervin Bibby. He was not in Des Moines during the debate but the legislators knew about him all too well.

Bibby ran a gas station a few feet over the Missouri line on Highway 69 four miles south of Lamoni, Iowa. He sold from 250 to more than 300 pounds of yellow oleo a day (1,800 to 2,400 pounds a week). Iowans flocked by the hundreds to the station and to similar outlets all along the Missouri border.

Iowa merchants didn't hide their pain. Said H.A. Reynolds, Hy-Vee food store manager at Lamoni, "So far as oleo is concerned, I just don't have any business at all." He was charging 43 cents a pound for uncolored oleo; Bibby was getting 35 to 38 cents for yellow oleo.

Bibby, a onetime Iowa farmer, had so much business he didn't want any more. "Me and the woman has worked hard," he said. He also was selling a lot of gasoline and cigarettes due to the fact that Missouri taxes were lower than those of Iowa. But the oleo situation seemed to bother Iowa managers the most. Reynolds commented, "We have an oleo law that is really driving cash into neighboring states."

As the oleo tensions heightened, butter forces declared all they were trying to do was to protect the consumer from getting cheated. The Iowa State Dairy Association said customers might get yellow oleo when they thought they were buying butter. Representative George Paul of Brooklyn, Iowa, said yellow oleo in the stores would lead to "widespread fraud" against the shopper.

In the name of protection against fraud, the butter people came up with a geometric amendment. They sought to require manufacturers to package oleo in quarter-pound pieces that were triangular rather than rectangular in shape. That way, they said, the housewife would know for sure what she was buying.

Representative Gladys S. Nelson of Newton, Iowa, didn't go for the triangle idea at all. She was the only woman in the Legislature and a strong leader of the pro-oleo forces. Housewives were perfectly capable of reading labels on oleo boxes, she said, then added, "It would be just as ridiculous to require beet sugar and nylon hose to be sold in triangular packages to protect the consumer who might confuse them with cane sugar and silk hose."

Representative Fred Schwengel of Davenport said of triangular oleo, "How silly will that make the state of Iowa look!"

There were nearly 15,000 persons in Iowa state prisons, mental hospitals and homes at the time. All were getting butter with their meals. Representative Clifford Strawman of Anamosa, Iowa, demanded that they continue to be served butter. With considerable emotion, Strawman asked, "Do you want oleo forced on people who have no choice in what they eat? On people, many of whom can't read or write? Or are deaf and cannot see?"

Strawman's amendment won temporary approval but finally was dropped from the bill. Before long, those institution people were eating cheaper oleo, with no reported ill effects.

The butter legislators stormed at the oleo coalition as the bill neared the final vote. The harsh language drew reprimands from Speaker William Lynes in the House of Representatives.

Representative Paul charged, "The oleo cartel, which has poured thousands of dollars in this effort to pick us off like a sitting duck, will laugh at the apathy, the coldness, the insensibility, the indifference, yes, even the stupidity of the Iowa farmer."

GLADYS S. NELSON
of Newton
Iowa Official Register 1953-54

Speaker Lynes broke in to say, "Please refrain from those remarks or you will be seated."

Representative Gus Kuester of Griswold didn't draw fire when he denounced "the slimy hands of greed by some interests who reach out for gain regardless of who is injured." But Representative Lawrence Putney of Gladbrook got a verbal spanking when he mentioned Mickey Jelke. Mickey was an heir to the Jelke fortune which was based on the popular Jelke brand of oleo. Mickey had gotten involved in an eastern national scandal that made juicy reading in the newspapers.

"You have all read about Mr. Jelke," began Putney.

"The gentleman is out of order in mentioning that name," the Speaker said sharply.

Putney nevertheless went on, "Did you ever hear of a dairyman's son or the son of a butter manufacturer cavorting around New York City?"

That salvo, condemning the actions of an oleo heir and exalting the morals of butter young people, was about the last shot fired in the legislative oleo battle. The issue came to a vote in both houses soon after. It wasn't even close.

Yellow oleo in the package won on a 40-8 vote in the Senate and 92-12 in the House. The oleomargarine war of 1953 was over.

God Help Us All!

Mayo Buckner had a quick mind. His IQ of 120 was better than the average of the population generally. Yet Mayo was forced to spend nearly his whole life as a patient in the state institution for the mentally retarded at Glenwood, Iowa.

He was taken there in 1898 as an 8-year-old boy. The *Des Moines Register* brought his story to national attention 58 years later, in 1956, when he was 66.

It was a horrible mistake to dump a little, intelligent human being into such an institution and leave him there for generations. Iowa Governor Herschel Loveless called it "a shame on humanity." There were 1,800 patients in Glenwood at the time.

The revelation of how Mayo had been wronged might have been expected to lead to immediate freedom. But that was not to be. Mayo could not accept various outside job offers because of diabetes. He lived out his remaining years in the institution. Death came at 74 years of age in 1964.

The publicity did lead to release of several others who also never should have been kept in Glenwood. None had a mind equal to that of Buckner, however.

How institution officials could have failed over the years to return Mayo to normal life is a mystery of the century.

Evidence of his brightness was everywhere in the institution. He subscribed to and read *Time* magazine and the *Omaha World-Herald.* He developed into a proficient printer and took over as foreman of the institution's print shop. He proved to be musically gifted. He learned to play eight instruments. He directed the institution band at times. He played in the Glenwood town band. He gave cornet lessons to an institution official. He gave piano lessons to town children. He was described as an excellent music teacher.

MAYO BUCKNER

All this in a person who was inexplicably classed as a "medium grade imbecile" when he was committed as a small boy. Such an imbecile has an IQ of less than 40.

It appears that superstition pushed Mayo into Glenwood in the first place. The Buckner family lived in Lenox in southern Iowa. Mr. Buckner was a carpenter. Mrs. Buckner was pregnant with Mayo in 1890 when she went to see "Blind Boone," a famous traveling blind piano player. Somehow she got the notion that Boone had put a "birthmark" (or hex) on her unborn child. She feared from the first her son was not right. She said in the Glenwood application to admit Mayo that he "rolled his eyes and made peculiar noises in exact imitation of blind Boone."

Reading the application in its entirety makes one wonder why Glenwood authorities ever accepted Mayo.

The mother wrote:

> This child is not foolish but is lacking in many ways. I do not wish to send him to public school for he will not protect himself but will take any amount of ill usage and never mention it.
>
> I think he needs special management and I am unable to undertake it. I think this is the place for him. Have talked with our Dr. A.W. Fees and he thinks so too.

The rest of the application indicates that Mayo was a sensitive and musically inclined lad. Here are some of the questions and answers (note that Mayo is sometimes referred to in the questions as "it" rather than "he"):

Is the child truthful? Perfectly.

Is it inclined to run away? Not now. Used to at 4 or 5 years of age. Would now I suppose if not well controlled.

Does it realize the difference between right and wrong? In some ways I think he will almost invariably say he has done anything whether he has or not. . . .

Does it behave properly at the table? Eats too fast and takes too much at one mouthful, about as other children do.

What is its general health? Good. Still, he is delicate. Excitement will make him pale and out of sorts. When a baby, he was very nervous and when we would go away from home, if it wasn't quiet, he would invariably have a sick spell which the doctor would call simple nervous fever.

The mother described little Mayo as rather prying and likes to know what is here and there, he was not obedient for the training he has had.

Is it good tempered? He is quite good tempered compared with others. Is it cruel? No, tender. Is it abusive to other children? Not at all but will stand abuse quietly.

And does this sound retarded? "Is the memory good? Yes, very, to learn verses or something others are learning, letters, spelling, etc." And on music: "Can it sing? Yes. Can play with one hand on organ any tune he hears. Plays the French harp nicely."

There were other early signs of Mayo's mental and musical ability. A 1905 institution teacher's report said of 15-year-old Mayo: "[He] does good work in school. Reads well and understands. In number work he is doing long division and fractions. Does good work in singing class. In drawing does quick and artistic work. Plays first violin in the orchestra." First violin!

All of which doesn't sound like a report on a longtime patient in an institution for the mentally retarded.

In adulthood, Mayo was a gentle, soft-spoken man, 5 feet 6 inches tall, weighing 140 pounds. He remembered clearly being brought to Glenwood.

"My mother and I came on the train," he said. "It was a snowy October day. The train had coal oil lamps. I didn't understand

GLENWOOD STATE INSTITUTION BAND

what was happening. I was looking forward as best I could."

His parents came to see him "once or twice a year." Occasionally they took him home in the summertime. They always brought him back.

Deeply moved by the 1956 disclosure of Mayo's case was his younger sister, Mrs. Clarence Ver Steeg of Victorville, California. Mrs. Ver Steeg, 54, visited Mayo several times over the years.

"I have known fine men in my life," she said. "He is one of the finest I have ever known. There is no meanness or dishonesty about him."

She said that Mayo being in Glenwood "was always a sorrow in our family."

"Mother was very heavy-hearted," the sister said. "We thought Mayo was different. Maybe he is finer and more sensitive than the rest. We never questioned why he was in Glenwood."

Asked if she thought that her brother might have been cheated out of having a family and home of his own, Mrs. Ver Steeg said, "To me Mayo is perhaps in a small way a musical genius. Music has been his wife and children. I believe his life has been very full. He has not made any money, it is true. But if life is measured by doing things a person wants to do, then Mayo has been a happy man."

When it was pointed out that Mayo might have had a notable career in music in normal life, the sister said tearfully, "If that is true, then God help us all! If that is true, then it is a pity and a tragedy."

Mayo himself loved the attention and acclaim from the 1956 exposé.

"I never realized I shouldn't be here before you talked to me about it," he told a *Register* reporter.

He enjoyed having a *Life* magazine team come and produce a big story about him. He loved getting a lot of mail, including a $1,000 check from a New York attorney and an offer of a new clarinet from an instrument company. He couldn't leave the institution because diabetes had forced amputation of his left leg below the knee. In a couple of years, he had to give up playing the violin too because of an ailing wrist but he continued performing on the clarinet, flute, saxophone and cello. He liked to read fiction but not if the stories were about killing. He was asked, "If you had your choice of where to go and what to do, what would you select?" "I would like to go where there was a good orchestra or band," he replied, "and sit and listen."

Less spectacular, but still poignant, were the stories of other "normal" patients who never should have been in Glenwood.

Alfred Sasser was the new superintendent in 1956. He had been there but six months. He was frank in describing conditions as he found them. He said there were at least 178 patients with IQs of 70 or higher. He added that as a general rule, persons above 70 do not need to be in an institution.

Sasser cited Lee Swearengin, 58, of Des Moines. Swearengin

had been a patient since 1910, or for 47 years. His older brother, Carl, was received at the same time. Both were listed as "medium grade imbeciles." Which had to be flat wrong. Sasser said Lee was found in the 1950s to have an IQ of 95. The normal range is 90 to 110. Carl's IQ must have been at least as high or higher. Carl escaped from Glenwood in 1918 and joined the navy in World War I. He became a cornetist in the famed John Philip Sousa band. After the war he played in bands around the nation. In World War II, he worked as an inspector in West Coast yards building ships. He certainly was no mental cripple.

Lee Swearengin also was a musician. He played the accordion and was a drummer. The Glenwood music director said in his 1950 report that "Lee's musicianship is of the highest caliber. He reads everything in sight. His rhythm is very good. He is fine to work with."

Lee was asked in an interview whether he missed not having had a lifetime with a family of his own. "It is too late now," he replied. "After you get older, you forget about such things."

He recalled his father and stepmother bringing him to Glenwood back in 1910. As a 10-year-old boy, he said he had no inkling what was happening. "I felt bad when they went away and left me," he said. He cried.

It is likely that Lee and Carl ended up in Glenwood, not because of lack of mental ability but because of strife between their father and stepmother. Lee said she served notice on the father to get rid of the boys, that she didn't want them around. So to Glenwood they were railroaded.

Lee recalled that when he was young, Glenwood patients frequently were whipped with straps but that had been stopped years before.

Lee was 6 feet 2 inches tall and weighed 180 pounds but was hesitant and timid. He came to Des Moines to work after release but had a hard time adjusting to outside life. He had an enormous amount of everyday living to learn. He didn't know, for example, how to dial a phone or the meaning of green, yellow and red in stoplights. He finally was placed in a maintenance job at a nursing home in Perry, Iowa, where he was a beloved person. He died in the 1980s.

Seth Perkins, 44, was released in 1957 after 25 years in Glenwood. An early record placed his mentality as that of a low grade moron. A later test, however, gave him a rating of at least 80. He had gone through eight grades in the Des Moines schools.

Seth got a job as a janitor in the state capitol complex and performed well until retirement.

It is likely that Seth was another victim of an unhappy home and was classed as retarded only for somebody's convenience. His record said: "His mother is dead and his father refuses to pay any attention to him. The boy is very kindly mannered and courteous but refuses to obey the persons with whom he is placed." Hence, to Glenwood he went.

Sasser said the people had to realize that institutions such as Glenwood shouldn't be used as repositories "to run away from human problems." He added: "When you don't have qualified professional help and services [in such an institution], individuals can get lost in a sea of human beings."

Wingless Chickens

I n the grand scheme of things, the chicken always has had two wings.

Peter Baumann of Urbandale, Iowa, changed that. He disclosed in 1949 that he had bred a wingless chicken. He displayed a flock of several hundred such birds, created by 12 years of inter-breeding freak specimens.

His achievement excited nationwide interest. The public was intrigued by the possibility of a better dinner table chicken and also one that couldn't escape the coop by flying over the fence.

The elated Baumann said his new chicken "dressed out beautifully, with more white meat where the wings are on other birds. Who likes wings anyway?" He declared the "airplane characteristics of a usual chicken are obsolete."

Baumann was a 33-year-old onetime Iowa farm boy who sold hatchery and veterinary supplies in Texas first, then in Iowa. He had been interested in genetics, the science of heredity, since his student days at Iowa State University in Ames.

For years hatchery operators saved malformed chicks for Peter, those born with a stub of one wing, for example, or some other abnormality.

Baumann conceded that he got a lucky break in his experiments. In the late 1930s he was given a light Brahma rooster and a white Minorca hen, both with stubs for wings. Later he got a black Austerlof hen, also with stubs.

He, of course, didn't know what he was going to get when he started breeding them. One of the first arrivals was a wingless chick. He was as amazed as anybody.

"Somewhere back in the ancestry of one of those chickens was this wingless tendency," he said. "Something like that might not happen again in 100 million hatchlings."

The idea after that was to use only wingless chickens in breeding, as they became available.

The fertility wasn't good at first. Out of a hatch of 70 eggs in an incubator, he got perhaps only eight chicks, two wingless. Then things picked up. He got as many as 15 chicks out of a hatch and three or four were wingless.

He moved back to Iowa in the middle of his experimental work and settled in Urbandale, a suburb of Des Moines. He traveled as a salesman in Iowa and part of South Dakota. The chicken breeding was a sideline that took up his weekends and evenings when in town.

To speed up the wingless development, he segregated the birds into family groups, each consisting of one rooster and four hens. For years Baumann followed an almost endless routine of hatching out batches of chicks, collecting eggs for breeding stock, raising the selected birds, collecting their eggs, then hatching out other batches, and so on.

Though the wingless "race" started as Light Brahma–White Minorca in color, they mostly looked like White Leghorns in Baumann's last flock. That was because he had bred the wingless strain into White Leghorn birds. He did so in an effort to improve the egg production. But he never did come up with figures showing that wingless hens laid any more eggs than their flapping cousins. He did say once, wishfully perhaps: "What about all the energy ordinary birds waste in useless flapping and flying about? That energy can be utilized in the production of meat and eggs."

He continued to get and use chicks with stub wings, with one full wing and a stub wing, and sometimes with a full wing on one side and nothing at all on the other. He kept those separate from the wingless birds.

The wingless chickens looked no different in a flock from their normal relatives. Closer examination, however, showed their sides to be somewhat depressed where the wings should have been.

Baumann couldn't estimate how much money and time he had invested in the project other than to say it was "plenty." In 1949, he said he was spending $200 a month for feed and to pay a teenage assistant.

Iowans got a good look at the wingless birds when Baumann brought some to the State Fair.

Baumann was dubious at first about selling any of his chickens. If he sold a pair, he said, "that would mean I have a competitor." However, he did sell some at $300 a pair and finally sold the entire operation, birds and all, to a Texas outfit. He never disclosed the sale price.

Baumann heard afterwards that some birds had died in Texas "but I really can't tell you what happened to all of them." There was no word on their fate decades later either.

Baumann and others saw a great future at one time for worldwide marketing of wingless chickens. It was felt that cooks would have welcomed not having to pay for wings that were nearly all bone. Also, it appeared that wingless birds would be easier to pluck, clean and store. But such purported advantages didn't build a market. The wingless birds did not revolutionize the chicken industry. If anybody made any appreciable money from them, it isn't known today.

One of the problems Baumann battled for years in his experimenting was the fact that the wingless rooster had all kinds of trouble mating. The usual rooster maintains its balance on the hen by flapping its wings. Baumann handled that difficulty at first by artificially inseminating the hens. Later, he said, the problem handled itself as more aggressive roosters learned to do the necessary balancing act.

One question that never was answered: Could a rooster get any satisfaction out of crowing at dawn and waking people up if it had no wings to flap in accompaniment? Baumann didn't know.

Leachman, Stick Around

At 20 years of age, glamorous Cloris Leachman competed for the 1946 Miss America title in Atlantic City, New Jersey. At 63, she delivered a tremendous performance in 1989 as old-lady "Grandma Moses" on the American stage.

In the intervening years, Cloris captured an Oscar in the movies and six Emmys in television, plus other awards. She had become one of the nation's brightest stars of screen, TV and the theater.

It all grew out of the dreams and determination of a talented Des Moines high school girl.

Cloris was only 15 when she joined the old Des Moines Kendall Community Playhouse. "Everything, I think, dated from there," she said. She got into three Kendall plays, one of which was *Ah, Wilderness,* Eugene O'Neill's only comedy.

Somebody saw the youngster at Kendall and got her a summer scholarship in radio at Northwestern University.

In 1943 Warner Brothers of Hollywood paid 17-year-old Cloris $20 to do a movie scene. A Warner company was at Fort Des Moines Army Post shooting a movie on the WACs (Women's Army Corps.)

"She was excellent," an assistant director said of Cloris. "She came through with flying colors."

By the time she was 18, she had had three radio programs of her own on stations KRNT and KSO, Des Moines. She read the *Des Moines Register* Sunday comics on the air. She reported on women in the news. And under the name Sara Wallace, she gave advice to housewives.

"Most of the housewives [listeners] were old enough to be her mother," said one report, "and one of them was."

Some of Cloris' early ability to express herself came from her mother. The family would be sitting around and the mother would suddenly say: "Cloris, sparkle!" And the little girl would "bat her eyes and smile brightly."

After graduating from Roosevelt High School in 1944, Cloris enrolled as a full-time student at Northwestern. She did so under a scholarship set up by Edgar Bergen, the famed "Charlie McCarthy" ventriloquist. In 1946 the Northwestern faculty voted sophomore Cloris "the most distinguished actress on the campus."

A group of judges gave a critical once-over to each of the beautiful young women as they passed by. The judges faced a serious decision. They had to select "Miss Chicago," the big city's entry in the Miss America contest.

The judges named Cloris "Miss Chicago."

A high Atlantic City pageant official predicted Cloris would be the new Miss America. A Des Moines enthusiast bet $100 against $300 that she would win in the 50-girl field. She didn't, but she finished in the top five and was awarded a $1,000 scholarship, equivalent to $8,000 in 1990's money.

As she paraded slowly on the runway before the final vote, Cloris heard a voice: "Cloris, sparkle!" It was her mother calling from the wings. And sparkle Cloris did.

Incidentally, Gail Fitch of the old Fitch Shampoo Company in Des Moines was an important figure at the 1946 Atlantic City event. The company donated $5,000 to the Miss America scholarship fund.

Fitch was a major American toiletry in 1946. The company sponsored a prime-time national Sunday radio program featuring the "Fitch Bandwagon." "Use your head, save your hair, use Fitch shampoo" was a familiar jingle nationwide.

Thus, it was no wonder that a titter ran through the pageant crowd of 20,000 when Gail was introduced. His hair was obviously thin. The shampoo hadn't done a good job of saving his hair.

Cloris scored high in both the swimsuit and talent competition but failed to win either. She showed her versatility by singing, dancing, acting, and playing the piano. The consensus was that she would have been better advised to have concentrated on one or two fields rather than try to squeeze four performances into her allotted three minutes.

Bess Myerson was the 1945 Miss America. She thus was the reigning queen at Atlantic City in 1946.

A tall and superbly beautiful woman, Bess was about the only glamour girl to whom reporters could talk freely. Under management rules, every Miss America hopeful was under guard of one or two vigilant chaperons at all times.

Every guy with a notebook and pencil was looked upon as a wolf in reporter's clothing.

The management said that if "the wrong kind of newsman gets to a girl, that can be very damaging to the girl and the pageant." Nobody worried about the damage that the young women might do to the press.

Still, it was fun for this author to be away for a while viewing the color and frills of Atlantic City instead of having to write about such critical things as taxation and how Iowa highway money was spent.

To be sure, there were crises, too, in Atlantic City.

Miss Cincinnati sat on some lipstick and got red all over the bottom of her white swimsuit shortly before it was her turn to parade before the throng. A frantic call went out for another swimsuit. Somebody quickly found one of suitable size. Miss Cincinnati was able to walk without a blemish on her posterior.

Jacqueline Means of Des Moines, the Miss Iowa entry, had a similar problem. She had a chigger bite ominously red in a wrong place. Luckily, wearing a one-piece swimming suit shielded that defect from the eagle eyes of the judges.

Jacqueline performed well as an acrobatic dancer but didn't reach the finals.

Cloris didn't go back to Northwestern for her junior year. Instead, she went to New York, "I thought for three days, with $60 in my pocketbook." Instead, she picked up three weeks work as an extra.

"In those days I earned $7 a day doing New York TV," she recalled. An agent steered her to a Rodgers and Hammerstein play in the making. Twenty-five young women competed for the opening.

"I was the second girl to read," Cloris said. "I did p-p-pretty well—Rodgers and Hammerstein and Irving Berlin were down in front listening. I thought uuhhhhh!"

She was called back for a second reading. "I didn't think I read as well the second time. I was awfully worried."

But out of the darkness beyond the lights came these thrilling words: "Leachman, stick around!"

She had landed a job to understudy the lead in the play. She had gotten a toehold in the Big Time.

A vast, energetic and rewarding life started unfolding for Cloris. Rarely if ever after that was she under any pressure of impending failure. In 1952, she commented: "I have been in New York six long luxurious years. No pounding pavements, not much knocking on doors. Never missed a meal." (Which few young stage hopefuls coming to the big city could say.)

Radio, stage, television, the movies—she was in all of them. And often it was high prestige stuff. She appeared in 1949 on the stage with Katharine Hepburn in Shakespeare's *As You Like It.* Cloris played Celia, Hepburn's cousin and pal. A newspaper review said Cloris "established herself as an actress of quality in a play of quality and almost at the beginning of her career."

Iowans saw Cloris in 1950 over WOI-TV Ames in a network dramatization of *Sense and Sensibility,* a Jane Austen classic. And Cloris starred in 1951 in Somerset Maugham's *Of Human Bondage* over NBC. *Billboard* magazine said she turned in a "stunning" performance as "a chippie who winds up as a frowsy blowzy rumpot. . . . She brought a sense of intense drama to the program and did a completely compelling job." A 1952 newspaper report said: "In the last two years, Cloris has been in virtually every TV dramatic show, such as 'Suspense,' 'Danger,' and 'Studio One.'"

Popular comedians Bob and Ray chose Cloris in 1952 when they needed a new woman for their NBC-TV show.

That same year she burst into major new prominence by singing the lead in the famous musical *South Pacific* for four weeks. She assumed the role of nurse Nellie Forbush and sang with zest such top songs as "I'm Gonna Wash That Man Right out of My Hair." (The regular star had gone on vacation.)

"Miss Leachman has the sense of comedy needed for such songs," said composer Richard Rodgers. "She delighted the audiences, especially in her comedy scenes."

Cloris wed director-producer George Englund in 1953 in what worked into an offbeat 25-year relationship. They had what they called "an open marriage." They maintained separate residences at least part of the time. They moved to the Hollywood area of California in 1954.

Four sons and a daughter were born to Cloris over a 13-year period. She stayed with her acting and was a good mother as well.

In 1954 Cloris took a major role on stage in the play *King of Hearts.* She played secretary to a maniacal comic-strip artist who drove everybody crazy. The secretary fell in love with him and wanted to marry him. She didn't and everybody escaped damage in the end. Brooks Atkinson, the *New York Times* critic, wrote: "As secretary, Cloris Leachman looks more beautiful than ever and acts with suppleness and variety."

At one point Cloris spent a full season as the mother of the boy who owned Lassie, the famous collie. She left the show even though it achieved a top TV rating. In effect, she became Lassie's mother. She said, "I got the feeling I was looking like the dog, so I quit."

By 1955 she had had another baby. She kept doing TV shows. In fact, she took her second son of three months with her daily to the set and nursed him between takes.

"I don't believe in bottle fed babies," she declared. She insisted that nursed babies "have a better start on life. It gives them a greater sense of security, and it gives them a better psychological foundation for the woes of this old world. All kids are going to be neurotic enough when they grow up. I feel you might as well give them all the security you can when they're young."

She said nursing is better physically for the child because mother's milk has "a lot of anti-bodies that cow's milk doesn't have." And "look at what a wonderful chance you have to cuddle the baby and give him added affection instead of turning him over to a nurse. Not only that, there's no messing around with formula far into the night."

She declared her home life was "more important than acting anyway."

"I love children," she said, "and I never feel they tie me down or that I am giving up anything to be with them."

But doesn't nursing a child cost a woman her figure? "That's silly," she said. "I've nursed both my babies and my figure is better than ever."

Her versatility as a performer was a matter of comment. "She plays everything from slapstick to high drama," wrote one critic, "and occasionally sings for her supper in a clear, well-trained soprano that brought her a Broadway lead the first time she ever auditioned with it." (Presumably the time when she sang the lead in *South Pacific*.)

Cloris didn't let up much as the years rolled by. She starred in 1959 as Sara Melody in the Eugene O'Neill play *A Touch of the Poet*. In 1968 she completed four TV shows. In "Judd for the Defense," she played the wife of an alcoholic judge who takes it out on defendants brought before him on liquor charges.

Why did Cloris Leachman do so well? What is her secret? Critic Joan Bunke of the *Des Moines Register* said her "first-class acting is in the details."

"Any movie goer or TV watcher who has seen Leachman at work," Bunke said, "knows that the richness, the liveliness, the individuality of her characters come from the details she puts into them, just as much from the physicality she gives them as from the lines of dialogue they speak."

The 1970s were a time of major triumph and of anguish for Cloris.

In 1972 she won that ultimate movie prize, the Academy Award, known as an Oscar, for best supporting actress in *The Last Picture Show.* She played the role of Ruth Popper, a sexually troubled, lonesome wife of a football coach. She goes to bed with a young man who later dumps her.

Cloris's performance was powerful because she put so much into the part. "I want to be inside people because then I can see myself," she said. "Ruth Popper is part of me now."

Amazingly, she captured six Emmys in television in the same general period (1970-1977). Four TV honors were awarded for performances as Phyllis Lindstrom, the slightly nutty neighbor of Mary Tyler Moore in the Moore serial show. Two more Emmys came for her work in "Phyllis," a later spinoff from the "Mary Tyler Moore Show."

And that wasn't all. In 1974, she gave a strong performance in *The Migrants,* a Tennessee Williams play. In 1975, she starred in a somber, gripping ABC movie of the week, *Someone I Touched.* That same year a writer commented: "In the movies these days you can see her [Cloris], not only in the Mel Brooks' spoof of the horror genre but also lending class in 'Daisy Miller' [the Henry James classic]."

She was a happy mother whose life was devastated when she learned her husband was playing around with another woman.

Cloris should have been prepared. After all, they had been separated since 1974. Nevertheless she was stunned in 1978 when husband George Englund divorced her for a younger woman.

Cloris put up a brave front of sorts at first.

"I am not a hungry or a desperate woman," she told a newsman in 1979. "I'm past needing a body in the house."

But the pain couldn't be repressed.

"I always wanted to be George's onlyest," she admitted. "His little darling."

She objected to the term "ex-husband": "You can't 'ex' out a husband of 25 years." And she tried to sound generous toward the new woman: "Bonnie, that's her name, is delightful. And so pretty. She honors and respects me, so why should I resent her?"

But when asked what she really thought of George taking up with Bonnie, Cloris burst out:

> I hate it! It's that dammed storybook ending that kills us all. I wanted what I had with George to be more than it was. I wasn't content with the status quo.
>
> They say that divorce is tough. They're crazy. It's marriage that's a bitch.

Somebody should write a real-life drama called *Cloris.* It could be a good one.

Liquor by the Drink

P hil Roan was a guy with a big cigar and a genial disposition. He gained a measure of fame by having boxed bottles of Scotch whisky stacked up like cordwood in his hotel room in downtown Des Moines.

Many people came. They drank. The Scotch pile sank lower and lower. But Phil didn't achieve his purpose, which was to help get the Iowa liquor law changed by plying legislators with free drinks.

Roan was a Fort Madison, Iowa, attorney. He served as a State Representative in the Iowa Legislatures of 1935, 1937 and 1939.

Iowa law at the time prohibited sale of liquor by the drink. You couldn't walk into a place and legally buy a mixed drink or a shot of whisky over the bar, or a drink of wine either—only beer with a limit of 3.2 percent alcohol. The only legal way to get the "hard" stuff was to buy a whole bottle at a state liquor store.

Despite the law, many places around the state sold liquor by the glass anyway.

Liquor forces, notably hotels and big out-of-state distillers and their salesmen, wanted liquor-by-the-drink legalized to increase their sales volume. The industry set up a secret fund to lobby a liquor-by-the-drink bill through the 1939 Legislature.

Coming as he did from a "wet" Mississippi River city, Roan played an important role in the liquor drive. He poured a lot of Scotch in his room, which was 501 in the Hotel Kirkwood. More important, he was chairman of the Liquor Control Committee of the House of Representatives. He saw to it that the committee introduced a liquor-by-the-drink bill.

The free Scotch drew a wide variety of visitors. Drinking lawmakers dropped by for a snort. So did lobbyists, visitors, hangers-on, and members of the press. (Roan's wasn't the only such room. Other lobbies with bills to pass or defeat maintained so-called "wet" rooms in hotels around the Des Moines loop as well.)

Liquor forces tried to make their bill palatable to the "drys." One section provided for "local option," that is, to allow a community to ban the sale of liquor by voting it down in an election if it so desired.

But that didn't help the liquor cause. The bill suffered a crushing defeat in the House. It was tabled (killed) by an 84-21 vote. The issue didn't get anywhere in the Senate either. Lined up against the measure were such potent "dry" groups as the Methodists, with a thousand churches in the state, and the Women's Christian Temperance Union (WCTU). Also opposed were moderates who believed liquor was sufficiently obtainable by the bottle in state stores and there was no need for a by-the-drink law.

The defeat wasn't all that unexpected. A similar Roan proposal in 1937 was beaten even worse, 90-16.

Roan never was apologetic. He told the Legislature that such a bill was "a law enforcement measure. You criticize lax law enforcement in your cities and yet you won't give them the money ît takes to enforce state laws that the state itself is not enforcing." He said money from licensing establishments would provide much needed enforcement cash to local governments.

On the other side, dry Representative Earl Fishbaugh declared: "The hotel men have been flying around here like mongrel hounds on a rabbit's tail, and all of us know why. They think this bill will let them make more profit out of liquor than they do now."

The Iowa ban on liquor by the drink continued for 24 years after Roan's last session. Not until 1963 was the restriction repealed. That success, if it can be so called, probably was due in large part to intensive reporting by the *Des Moines Register.* The newspaper demonstrated in a 1962 statewide investigation how unworkable the law had become. A headline trumpeted:

"LIQUOR BY THE DRINK IN 2/3 OF IOWA."

Reporters traveled over 10,000 miles discovering how easy it was in a majority of counties to buy liquor by the drink in most taverns and clubs, contrary to law.

"Liquor was sold by the drink in counties containing at least 2.2 million of the state's 2.8 million population," the *Register* said. "It is doubtful whether any other state law ever was more widely ignored, except possibly the 25-year ban on sale of cigarettes from 1896 to 1921."

It wasn't the case of only big cities either. "Sale has been more or less commonplace even in small towns of such counties as Dubuque, Scott, Woodbury, Clinton, Pottawattamie, Crawford, Carroll, Plymouth and others," the paper said.

The reporters failed to buy liquor by the drink in only 20 of the 99 counties. The status of the law in perhaps 10 other counties was uncertain. At least four counties were totally dry; Howard, Ringgold, Van Buren, and Wayne had no liquor by the drink, or state stores either.

"In most county seats you don't need your own bottle," the *Register* said. "All you need is the money, and courage to walk into a club and ask for a Bourbon, after telling the bartender you are sick of beer. You can have the Bourbon straight or mixed, or you can order a martini and Manhattan."

Iowans were jarred. They knew the law was being flouted but they hadn't realized how widespread the violations had become. The people decided to act. The result was an upheaval in the 1962 election and the 1963 Legislature.

Information on the sale of federal Retail Liquor Dealer permits (RLDs) proved helpful in uncovering the extent of the violations. Federal law required every establishment selling liquor to pay $54 a year for an RLD no matter what a state law might say. Federal records showed 1,784 Iowa private establishments bought RLDs in the 10 months beginning July 1, 1961. That was an average of 18 to the county. No Iowa operator was arrested for failing to have an RLD. All made sure to have them. They evidently were more afraid of federal than of state and local prosecutors.

Iowa clubs were big buyers of RLDs. Said the *Register,* "If you happen to be a member of the Elks, Eagles, Moose, American Legion, Amvets or Veterans of Foreign Wars, you don't often have to go thirsty. Drinks in many such places sell for 40 to 60 or 70 cents, depending on what you order." (You pay about that much for a plain Coke now.)

At least 87 American Legion posts obtained RLDs. So did 49 Veterans of Foreign Wars (VFW) posts, 43 Elks lodges, 30 Moose, 26 Eagles and 12 Amvets posts.

The City of Dubuque was the overall RLD champion of the state with 172 federal RLD permits. Davenport was second with 164, Sioux City third with 158 and Council Bluffs fourth with 87. Other totals included Clinton 77, Des Moines 52, Burlington 51, Keokuk 41, Muscatine 34, Fort Dodge 33, Fort Madison 29, Cedar Rapids 26, Carroll 24, Le Mars 19, West Des Moines 11 and Ottumwa 8.

"In some places getting into a club and buying liquor was easy," the newspaper reported. "Other clubs, however, enforce tight restrictions against non-members."

In Independence, "they were pouring liquor in a club as if it were not going to be here anymore." In Waukon, Iowa, a reporter was told, "This is Iowa. You can't buy a drink here." But in Coon Rapids, a reporter declared, "You can't tell me I can't buy a drink here." The woman bartender replied, "No, I'm not" as she poured him a drink. At Tiffin, a club was going full blast Saturday night. Anything you want.

But at Spirit Lake, even with your own bottle, a person was looked upon as if he were asking for life eternal when he wanted a setup. (A setup is a carbonated beverage in a glass into which liquor is mixed.) In Muscatine a report said only two of the city's dozens of taverns were not selling liquor by the drink "but this could not be verified."

Numerous Iowans enjoyed being part and parcel of breaking the law. They loved the air of mystery and intrigue. In

Shenandoah, for example, there was a bit of a thrill in this scenario: A reporter touched a button. There was a Bzzz! Whereupon the lock snapped and the door opened into a club where liquor was being sold by the drink.

It didn't quite work out that way in Audubon. There a bell sounded at the door of a club. A voice coming over the loud speaker asked for the visitor's identification, then said, "Sorry, for members only."

It took very little effort to gain entrance to other clubs. A payment of 25 cents qualified a reporter for membership in an Estherville club where he could drink, eat and dance if he wanted to. In Cedar Rapids, it cost $1 for a membership and the right to buy drinks. In Ottumwa you were automatically a member of a club in a hotel if you were registered in that hotel. In the Catholic town of Remsen, the taverns opened immediately after mass on Sunday mornings.

Enforcement was especially difficult along state borders on the Mississippi and Missouri rivers. That was because laws of all the states touching Iowa permitted sale of liquor by the drink. That was true in Wisconsin, Illinois, Missouri, Nebraska, South Dakota and Minnesota.

"The presence of liquor by the drink as close as the other end of a bridge has had the most profound effect," the *Register* said. "For example, Omaha, Nebraska [on the Missouri], where liquor flows freely, is right on Council Bluffs' doorstep. The result is a liquor-by-the-drink system in such Iowa counties, law or no law." Council Bluffs is in Pottawattamie County.

At Sioux City, also on the Missouri, "taverns, key clubs and fraternal clubs generally sell liquor by the drink," the *Register* reported. "Many kept liquor in pitchers that could be easily dumped" (in case of a raid).

There was no fear of local raids, however. Indeed, the Sioux City chief of police accompanied reporter Fred Pettid in making the rounds checking liquor-by-the-drink sales.

Pettid was an excellent reporter who could drink with anybody. He may have been the newsman assigned to Fort Dodge as well. Whoever that was, he visited seven Fort Dodge taverns, bought and presumably drank a highball in each.

Another reporter found bourbon whisky selling for 35 cents a shot in Dubuque, apparently the cheapest drink in the state.

Probably the most expensive was 95 cents for a "grasshopper" in Davenport. (How dirt cheap compared with today.) A Davenport bar featured a straight shot of whisky followed by an eight-ounce bottle of beer as a chaser, a combination known as a boilermaker.

The survey said liquor by the drink could be obtained "in dozens of Polk County places outside Des Moines and in the city if you know the right people." One suburban Polk County bartender served drinks from his pants pockets. He carried a half-pint bottle of bourbon on one hip and an equal amount of Scotch on the other.

A reporter got his comeuppance in the Humboldt County town of Livermore. He ordered a drink. The bartender shoved a glass of water at him and said: "Five cents please." The reporter asked where the bourbon was. The bartender said he didn't have any.

Incidentally, the *Register* stressed the fact that finding liquor on sale by the drink in one or two places in a county didn't mean the practice was prevalent all over the county. Other towns in the county may not have permitted such sales at all.

These questions naturally came up: How come local officials allowed so many violations? Were they paid off?

Part of the answer lay in the fact that people in many communities wanted liquor sold by the drink, or didn't care one way or the other. Business forces in Des Moines, for example, favored an "open town." They wanted the city to be a place where Iowans could come and "relax." Thus, local officials were often not under pressure to enforce the law.

As to payoffs, they probably took place, although the *Register* probe didn't go into that. In an unnamed county, though, it was learned that an establishment operator told the sheriff in a meeting, "After all the money we kicked into your campaign, you aren't going to turn around and put the heat on us, are you?" The sheriff said, "Shush, there's a reporter present."

Campaign contributions were not necessarily payoffs, although they could have been. There was no way to tell in those days. There was little honest reporting of campaign receipts and expenditures. A candidate could spend the money for political purposes or he could use it to pay personal bills, his monthly home mortgage payment maybe.

One somewhat surprising discovery: The reporters found that

quite a number of illegal operators didn't want a liquor-by-the-drink law enacted. They liked things the way they were. They feared a new law would limit the number of licensed establishments in a town and some would have to go out of business. They also didn't want to have to pay expected high license fees. But they were not a majority.

The *Register* disturbed many usually "dry" Republicans. They didn't want the liquor situation to upset the status quo. The Republicans were the majority party in the state.

"The Republicans do pretty well in many of the wetter counties along the big rivers," the *Register* said. "The party wants to hold that strength, particularly since the Republican edge statewide over the Democrats no longer is comfortable."

In addition, the Republicans long had gotten the biggest share of the vote in county seat towns. The party didn't want the attention on liquor to rile up the politics in those towns.

Republican fears were well-founded. Stories on the *Register* investigation appeared in newspapers of May 6 and 13, 1962. Six months later, Democrat Harold Hughes won an upset victory in the election race for governor. Hughes defeated Governor Norman Erbe of Boone, the Republican incumbent. The vote was Hughes 432,000, Erbe 389,000.

Hughes ran on an outright platform of legalizing liquor by the drink. He decried the widespread liquor violations and said the old-time saloon had returned on an illegal basis in most parts of the state. Erbe said, "Legal liquor by the drink would be a more efficient method of distribution" but he refused to say whether he would sign or veto such a bill. The directness of Hughes' position appealed to a majority of the voters.

The governorship was the Republicans' only major loss in 1962. The party won the U.S. Senate race, six of Iowa's seven seats in Congress, and all the other elective state offices, plus control of the 1963 Legislature.

The legislators got the message. They enacted a law legalizing liquor by the drink under county option. The measure provided for countywide elections on the by-the-drink question. The first such elections saw a number of counties voting for liquor by the drink and a few choosing to stay "dry."

In the ensuing years, the Legislature repealed the local option provision and eliminated the state liquor stores. Thus, Iowa entered the 1990s a wide-open liquor state, far afield from its reputation as a onetime citadel of dry sentiment.

Prayed for Notre Dame

J ohn F. Kennedy gracefully sidestepped a touchy question in a 1959 political visit to Iowa.

He was in the Midwest testing sentiment prior to his successful 1960 race for the presidency.

Kennedy took time out to attend a football game at Iowa City between the University of Iowa and Notre Dame. He was asked afterwards which team he favored. That kind of a question always puts a politician on the spot. If he had said Iowa the Notre Dame fans wouldn't have liked it, and vice versa. Kennedy escaped with this droll reply, "I cheered for Iowa, and prayed for Notre Dame." The prayers were answered. Notre Dame won a squeaker, 20-19.

Kennedy was a U.S. senator from Massachusetts at the time. He found himself in an unexpected row with Al Boss, operator of the Savery Hotel in Des Moines. Kennedy stayed at the Savery. Boss met Kennedy in a hallway and jumped all over him for sponsoring a bill in Congress to raise the minimum wage from $1 an hour to $1.20 an hour. (That's right, $1 to $1.20!)

Boss didn't object to the raise but to a provision to extend the minimum to five million additional people, including hotel workers. Boss didn't want to have to boost the pay of his employees. Kennedy politely stood his ground. The bill did pass but didn't go as far on hotel employees as Kennedy wanted.

In the 1960 race, Kennedy first had to win the nomination by gaining support of a majority of the delegates in the Democratic National Convention in Los Angeles. He naturally wanted the votes of as many Iowa delegates as possible.

Governor Herschel Loveless headed the Iowa delegation. The Kennedy forces sought to inveigle Loveless into believing that he was a possibility for the nomination for vice president. (The Kennedys used the same tactic with Governor Orville Freeman of Minnesota and Senator Stuart Symington of Missouri.)

Skeptics didn't believe Kennedy was sincere in telling Loveless that he might be chosen for vice president. But the governor took the bait and voted for Kennedy in the convention, as did most of the other Iowans. Kennedy was nominated on the first ballot.

As it happened, Kennedy passed over Loveless and the other two and named Senator Lyndon Johnson of Texas for the vice presidential spot. Kennedy made the announcement in a press conference. A reporter brought the news of the Johnson selection to Governor and Mrs. Loveless while they were eating lunch in a nearby hotel dining room.

The disbelieving Mrs. Loveless was furious at the reporter. "You shouldn't go around saying such things!" she declared. "I heard Jack Kennedy himself say it," the reporter responded.

Loveless called the choice "a real shocker" and the Kennedy-Johnson combination "a strange marriage."

HERSCHEL LOVELESS at the Iowa Statehouse

Many others in the Iowa delegation were dumfounded too. Delegate Don Harris of Bloomfield said reconciling Kennedy's liberal and Johnson's mostly conservative views would be impossible. Delegate Edris "Soapy" Owens, a Newton, Iowa, labor leader, said the one candidate he unalterably opposed was Johnson. Other Iowans said the Johnson selection meant Kennedy would lose Iowa and the farm belt to Richard Nixon, the Republican presidential nominee, in the fall election.

Political observers generally agreed that the Kennedy outlook in Iowa was bleak.

Kennedy sought to offset the pessimism in the campaign. Among other things, he tried to make a deal with a *Des Moines Register* reporter. Kennedy had paid for a private survey of Iowa by a noted pollster. The poll showed Kennedy had a chance to carry Iowa against Nixon. Kennedy told the reporter he could have the poll result for an exclusive story.

But the reporter noticed that the poll also showed Democrat Edward McManus would probably lose to Republican Norman Erbe in the race for governor of Iowa. Kennedy told the reporter he was not to write about the McManus-Erbe poll result, only the presidential part of the poll.

The reporter said both or nothing. Kennedy thereupon withdrew the story offer. The *Register* did not get to carry the poll story. The reporter said that limiting the story only to the portion favoring Kennedy would put the reporter in a position of being part of the Kennedy political organization rather than that of an independent newsman.

As it turned out, the poll wasn't accurate anyway. Kennedy lost Iowa to Nixon by a hefty 172,000 margin, considerably more than Erbe's 63,000 victory over McManus.

Loveless was the Iowa Democratic candidate for U.S. senator in the same election. His vice presidential dream may have harmed his candidacy. Observers felt that his concentration on trying to become Kennedy's running mate took a lot of steam out of his senatorial campaign. Loveless lost to Republican Jack Miller but the margin was only 47,000 votes, much better than Kennedy's 172,000 beating in Iowa.

As it worked out, Kennedy saved his own neck by selecting Lyndon Johnson for vice president. Kennedy won over Nixon in an extremely close race nationally. Without Johnson, Kennedy probably would have lost Texas and other southern states, and the election. Kennedy edged out Nixon in the popular vote by only 118,000 out of 68 million cast.

Kennedy said afterward that he never expected to have to find a job for Loveless in the national government, that he thought Loveless was a shoo-in for senator in Iowa. Kennedy did name Loveless chairman of a commission that renegotiated contracts with the defense industry for the government.

The Kennedy presidency created an aura of glamour around the White House. At 42, handsome John Kennedy was the youngest person ever to assume the presidency. First Lady Jackie was even younger (31) and a beautiful woman. They had two adorable little children.

There was no public knowledge as yet about Kennedy's womanizing to spoil the image. The press had always known about such goings-on involving presidents but didn't write about them.

Writers pictured the White House as a modern "Camelot." (The original Camelot was the legendary location of King Arthur's court in early England.) Kennedy was a beloved president of a lot of Americans.

Questions remained, however: Was John F. Kennedy for real politically? Was he any stronger with the voters than in 1960 when he barely escaped defeat? What were his chances of winning again in 1964?

Look magazine, circulation 7.5 million, sought answers in the fall of 1963, one year before the 1964 election. *Look* editors asked this author to conduct an intensive poll on the Kennedy outlook in a key Iowa precinct.

As political writer for the *Register,* I had done precinct polling in prior presidential campaigns. The polls had been accurate in indicating which way the political winds were blowing.

This time I sounded out 314 voters in rural Silver Lake Township of Palo Alto County in northwest Iowa. The Silver Lake precinct had "voted right" for president since 1896; that is, the precinct had given a majority of its votes to whoever was the presidential winner in every election beginning in 1896 and extending through 1960. Kennedy carried Silver Lake over Richard Nixon by 17 votes in 1960. The count was Kennedy 201, Nixon 184.

It was expected as early as 1963 that Barry Goldwater of

Arizona would be the 1964 Republican nominee for president. (Which he was.) The 1963 poll for *Look* sought to find out how Kennedy stood against Goldwater with Silver Lake voters. The result was Kennedy 148, Goldwater 141, George Romney of Michigan 2, and no opinion, 23. The voters were not asked about Romney but two volunteered support for him.

The danger to Kennedy and his slim 17 vote majority in 1960 showed up in the poll switches. Twenty-nine voters who supported Kennedy in 1960 said they leaned toward Goldwater in 1963. Fourteen who had voted for Nixon favored Kennedy in 1963, which indicated a preference loss of 15 for Kennedy.

The report concluded: "As of today, they [Silver Lake voters] give Kennedy a razor-edge majority. But with the slightest shift of mood, JFK could lose."

The *Look* story appeared in a late November issue of 1963. Over the story was a big headline: "JFK COULD LOSE." And on the front cover was another headline: "KENNEDY COULD LOSE."

As the world knows, an assassin's bullet killed President John F. Kennedy November 22, 1963. To the consternation of *Look* and myself, all copies of the magazine containing the fateful article had been printed and were starting to reach the newsstands.

Look tried to minimize the damage by pasting a new headline over the old one on the cover. But nothing could be done about the story spread over five pages inside the magazine.

Look publisher Gardner ("Mike") Cowles estimated that recalling and reprinting the magazine would have cost $10 million.

It was agonizing to have such a story come out, appearing to disparage a beloved president, at a time of national shock and mourning. *Look* received hundreds of angry letters. But it was a situation beyond anybody's control and of special deep regret, not only for the magazine but also for this author and the Iowans pictured and quoted in the article.

White Supremacy

S harp heavy axes wielded by hostile white prisoners cut the clothing and shoes of a quiet Iowan working on a road gang in North Carolina.

A dozen times the menacing axes nicked the skin and caused the blood to run.

At night he was unable to sleep much because he never knew when he would be roughed up in his bed by two or three prisoners. That happened, and the very unsympathetic guards did not interfere with the attackers very quickly.

Life was "a torment of insecurity."

It was a harrowing story of racial hatred and violence that the Reverend Waldo Mead told in 1962 upon returning to his native Cedar Rapids, Iowa. The 28-year-old Iowan was an ordained Methodist minister. He had been in Durham, North Carolina, two years, studying for a Ph.D. degree under full scholarship at Duke University. White supremacy still reigned in all its fury in the South.

The Iowan challenged that supremacy by trying to take a black friend into an all-white Durham restaurant. Mead was arrested for trespassing. He was brought before a judge who was a leading Methodist layman. Mead quoted the judge as saying:

Mr. Mead, I see you are a Methodist minister. The action you have taken makes me thoroughly ashamed of being a Methodist.

"We both have something to be ashamed of," Mead said. He was fined $25 and costs. Instead of paying the fine, he chose to go to jail. He found himself in the "drunk tank" with about 15 inebriated prisoners. When daylight came, he was placed in a prison road gang cutting brush and trees. The gang consisted of two "bullpens" of 52 men each. They all knew he was coming. The newspapers had carried the story of his arrest and conviction.

"The prisoners were very profane to me," he said.

The warden assigned Mead to what was called the "hell squad." He was put on the road with five other prisoners and a guard who had a shotgun in a nearby truck. Mead was given an area where the brush and trees were most difficult to cut.

> Men cut behind me and beside me. They would follow on my
> heels, cutting close to my feet and legs. They cut leather from
> my shoes. They nicked me up. They were accurate enough with
> the axes, which weighed maybe 15 pounds, to draw blood
> without causing serious injury. I was nicked perhaps a couple
> of dozen times.
>   The real problem was not the physical injury but the
> tension. You never knew when they might swing through.

In the long civil rights battles of the era, few if any other
Iowans had to endure such an ordeal.

He said that God "seemed pretty remote at times." The
"harassment and general enervation" was difficult to fight
psychologically. He "always realized the potentiality" of losing his
morale as he faced the possibility of being cut down by an axe.

A person feels at such time "the severity of the Cross, to put
it in theological terms." It was "all rather humbling" and sometimes
he felt presumptive to say that he was "representing the church"
and had the right to say "what the church should do."

He secretly kept a pencil, which was contraband in the prison.
He battled against the strain he was under by writing down his
thoughts and repeating Scriptures that he remembered.

One such Scripture was Galatians 4:28: "There is neither Jew
nor Greek, there is neither slave nor free, there is neither male nor
female, for you are all one in Christ Jesus." Mead said that verse
"gave me a sense of what I was in there for."

After 10 days, he decided to get out of prison by paying the
fine and costs. The total amount was close to $60. He had received
50 or 60 anonymous "hate letters" and several from friendly
sources containing upwards of $80 in cash.

He said his purpose in going to prison rather than paying the
fine immediately "was to convince the public, primarily the local
churches, of the nature and sincerity of my appeal." He added that
he did not seek "martyrdom," which would "only confuse the issues
which were already too easily confused."

Mead had gone public early in opposition to oppression of
blacks in the Durham area. He joined black organizations in
picketing segregated theaters and restaurants. He sought to
"persuade managers of certain restaurants" to serve blacks as well

as whites.

Mead was a graduate of Carleton College and Yale University Divinity School. A black friend from his Yale days came to visit him in Durham. Mead took the friend to a Methodist church. They were shunted into "a darkened balcony." Mead said that when they asked for a collection plate, the usher replied: "We don't serve Negroes."

After church the two went to a restaurant that was being picketed. Mead went inside and sat down. He said he told the waitress that he would order as soon as his friend was permitted to enter. He said he wanted to talk with the manager.

THE REVEREND WALDO MEAD
Courtesy of the Des Moines Register

The manager did not come, but the sheriff and a deputy did. They arrested Mead.

"I didn't resist, but I didn't cooperate either," he said. "I went 'limp.' Three men carried me out to a squad car."

While he was in custody, he succeeded in sending a letter to a Durham newspaper. The letter pleaded for recognition of man's universal brotherhood under God. He expressed objection to the preaching on Sunday morning of "the gospel of God's love to all men" and afterwards entering "a restaurant segregated with the protection of the law."

"One of the strangest lands of all is the church itself," he went on. "The church has become one of the least prophetic and least self-critical of all the areas of our society. In certain locations it has become a last refuge of the segregationists."

He didn't spare the North in his comments on the race problem. "I think we in the North express our prejudices and hatreds more subtly, more politely, and sometimes more cruelly than the southerners do," he observed.

Decline of the Bible Belt

B ack in the 1920s, H.L. Mencken derisively gave the name "Bible Belt" to the Deep South and such midwestern states as Iowa.

Satirist Mencken blasted fundamentalists and evangelicals in those states for believing in a literal interpretation of the Bible and in rigid morality. He held them responsible for prohibition, which outlawed the sale of liquor nationally from 1920 to 1933. He assailed their opposition to teaching evolution in the schools.

Similarly, Mencken branded the Baptists, Methodists, the Anti-Saloon League, and the Ku Klux Klan as "anti-intellectuals."

One Iowa historian wasn't surprised that Iowa was included in the Bible Belt. Ruth Gallaher of Iowa City, Iowa, wrote in 1933:

> It has been the custom of sophisticates to deride life in Iowa as uncouth, uncultured and narrow. Not so. Association with the soil is not uncouthness. Plain living does not of itself mean lack of culture. Morality is not a synonym of narrowness. Indeed, few states have been more tolerant of social and religious experience.

She described Iowans of her time as "fundamentally Anglo-Saxon, industrious, interested in religion and education, inventive, sturdy, and intelligent."

Another Iowa historian, Irving Richman of Muscatine, termed Iowa a "Corn and Bible Commonwealth" in 1931.

But by the 1990s, nobody would have called Iowa a Bible Commonwealth, or included it in the Bible Belt at all.

Within the span of one lifetime, sweeping changes had taken place in Iowa morals, mores, and manners. Especially was this true with regard to commercial gambling, the Sabbath, sexual freedom and liquor.

Here are some of the contrasts between the "old" and "new" Iowas.

The state constitution still banned lotteries and other forms of open gambling in the 1930s. That ban was repealed in 1972. The state itself began operating major lotteries in the 1980s and promotes them vigorously. Big gambling boats sailed the

Mississippi and Missouri rivers in 1992 under Iowa license. A picture of Governor Terry Branstad in front of a river boat slot machine appeared in the newspapers. (A picture of the head of state in such a location would have been beyond the comprehension of old time Iowans.) Betting on horse races takes place at the Prairie Meadows track near Des Moines. So does betting on dogs at Dubuque and Council Bluffs. (A Waterloo track battled money needs in mid-1994.) Native Americans operate big gambling casinos at Tama, Sloan, and Onawa, Iowa. Gambling bingo, where you pay to play and can win valuable prizes, has become lawful and commonplace.

The commandment "Remember the Sabbath day to keep it holy" lost much of its meaning. For generations big stores and nearly all little ones stayed closed Sundays. Now Sunday is a major shopping day. Movies couldn't show on Sunday in many cities and towns. That ban long since has disappeared. Many churches held both Sunday morning and evening services. It's nearly always morning only now.

GOVERNOR TERRY BRANSTAD tries the slot machines
Courtesy of the Quad City Times

Playing cards long was looked upon in many churches and homes as instruments of the devil. An evangelist named Bassett, preaching at a revival in the Baptist Temple at Marshalltown, shouted: "If any of you has a pack of cards and a Bible in your home, burn one of them up! They don't belong under the same roof. One is God's book and the other is the devil's book!"

Ballroom dancing was popular with the general public then, but not with many church leaders. Said the same evangelist:

> Folks have tried to reform the dance but they can't do it any more than they can reform a rattlesnake by clamping a clothespin on its tail. No young man can dance with a half-dressed girl and go home with prayer meeting thoughts.

Imagine what that evangelist's reaction would have been had he seen the words "dirty dancing" in a modern headline, accompanied by a picture of a couple in a suggestive embrace.

Whatever went on between the sexes in the 1930s, couples living together without marriage was not an accepted practice. Nor were pregnancies outside of marriage commonplace. Only illegal abortions were available. The birth-control pill hadn't been invented.

Even playing harmless amateur baseball on Sunday drew fire from church people who insisted that the day be used only for worship and rest. One Glenn Van Tuyl organized a team to play Sunday afternoons in the 1930s in the Scotch Ridge Presbyterian Church community in north Warren County. Pious church members sent him a petition saying:

> We believe you will agree that Sunday baseball is not in keeping with the ideals that have made this community what it is. We regret that you have seen fit to align yourself with any force that would tend to break down the principles for which the church stands.
>
> We protest Sabbath desecration and the use of the name "Scotch Ridge" by any group which does not respect the moral and spiritual values of those who spent their lives that we might have a respectable place in which to live and raise our families.

Van Tuyl gave up. No baseball was played at Scotch Ridge on

Sundays.

Gardner Cowles, Sr., was a stickler for what he regarded as cleanliness in a newspaper. He was the legendary publisher of the *Des Moines Register and Tribune* in the first half of the 20th century. Cowles under no circumstances would have permitted his papers to publish a 1991 picture captioned: "Barefoot, Pregnant— and Now Married." The picture showed three newly wed Ottumwa couples, with the bride-sisters all barefoot and admittedly pregnant. In the background stood the girls' father holding a shotgun!

Gardner Cowles, Jr., known as Mike and who was later publisher of the Des Moines papers, wrote things in his memoirs that his father never would have stood for. Mike told how actress Marilyn Monroe willingly allowed her breast to be exposed in his presence, and that the breast was unusual in that it pointed upward. Those details appeared in the newspaper.

Divorces were far less common in the early days. Iowa judges granted 4,144 divorces in 1931. The number soared to 10,939 in 1991. But it was more difficult to get a divorce half a century and more ago. You technically had to prove a specific cause such as "cruel and inhuman treatment." All it takes in the modern age is a witness to say merely that the differences between the husband and wife are irreconcilable.

Condoms were illegal in the earlier days but druggists were rarely if ever arrested for selling them. And earlier parents of students away at college would have gone out of their minds over a front-page story of recent years reporting the availability of condoms in vending machines in nine University of Iowa dormitories, and another story of condoms carrying the insignia of the university and of Iowa State University.

Even more disturbing to parents would have been photographs of packages of condoms in the 1988 Bettendorf school yearbook. And jarring indeed the 1991 recommendation of an Urbandale, Iowa, 13-year-old youth that schools should hand out condoms. The recommendation was displayed along with his picture in *U.S.A. Weekend,* nationwide Sunday newspaper magazine.

Such magazines as *Playboy* and *Penthouse* were still to come in the 1930s. So were explicit movies. Picturing a male and female wrestling in bed had not yet become routine. Sexy massage ads didn't appear in newspapers.

There were delicacies in public matters that may seem strange today. Reporters on many newspapers could not write that a person was accused of "rape." That was a no-no word. The reporter was limited to saying the individual faced "a statutory charge." Similarly, syphilis and gonorrhea could be referred to only as "social diseases."

Those words are a far cry from the gutter language that appeared in the *Register* September 13, 1992. Here was the situation: After a football game in Iowa City, Bret Bielema of the University of Iowa team told Iowa State Coach Jim Walden: "You have been a big prick. I've enjoyed kicking your ass the last five years." In his stunned reply, Walden said: "I don't think the last five years I have been an asshole."

Register sports columnist Marc Hansen was there. He reported the exchange as he heard it, naughty words and all. Readers erupted with a storm of letters. Writer Tom Lynner of Des Moines asked: "Is the *Register* saying our family values, at least on the language front, dipped so low that, so long as someone is being quoted, any word goes?"

Register editor Geneva Overholser replied:

> Our practice is to avoid offensive language except when it is essential to the story. Determining what is essential is the tough part. When do we need to give the readers the whole story, even if it includes a word that many will not like? We are not to the point that anything goes by any means. Yet the lay of the land on language usage is shifting quickly, which means the use-or-not-use profanity dilemmas come faster and faster for us.

It must be conceded that numerous readers did want to know exactly what was said and Hansen did satisfy that curiosity. Yet the appearance of such coarse words in a newspaper shocked many Iowans, and not all of them old timers.

But by 1994 frankness had progressed so far that the word "penis" in the headlines caused scarcely a ripple. What happened was an angry wife cut off her sleeping husband's penis. News stories described the act in explicit detail, which would have been far out of bounds in the old days.

Men were profane in everyday conversation way back, about like they are now but not often in the presence of women. A woman who used "bad words" where others could hear was rare. (How different now!) And never did we hear in those times anything to match the sweet young co-eds who chanted loud and clear: "One two three four, we don't want your f----- war." They directed their obscenity at visiting President Nixon at the Statehouse in Des Moines in the 1970s during the Vietnam conflict. The foul word, incidentally, didn't appear in the news reports of the occasion.

That Nixon confrontation also was notable for the fact that Iowa students (male) aimed a barrage of snowballs at the president. Perhaps that was the first time any president ever was snowballed. None hit him.

Topless barmaids in a small town tavern for even one night would have been unthinkable in the days of yore. Such a spectacle hasn't been unknown in Iowa in recent years and hasn't caused that much comment. Nor did a news story quoting a widely known actress as saying: "Marriage makes sex respectable, which then makes it unexciting." And an actor was quoted as complaining in Moscow because the Russians wouldn't let him take a woman to his hotel room to have sex.

And how was this for uninhibited news writing? "Got a backache? Try sex. Making love may release muscular constrictions, tone back muscles and relax the nervous system." Regularly prescribed back exercises "can be tedious for most while sex probably isn't. Research has found that an orgasm may have ten times the effect of the tranquilizer Valium."

An editor responsible for putting such material into a paper would have been fired right out the front door in the 1930s. He wouldn't have had time to get his hat. (Just about all men wore hats.)

A lot of Iowans in the bygone days hadn't accepted the fact of women smoking, and especially not in public. Cigarette manufacturers, though, bought a lot of advertising aimed at getting women to smoke. That irked Frank Pierce of Marshalltown, veteran legislative lobbyist for Iowa cities and towns.

"If, in order to stop the appeal to women and children to become smokers, it is necessary to prohibit the sale of cigarettes," Pierce said, "that is the thing that will surely happen in a majority of states." But it didn't happen. Pierce, however, did have an Iowa precedent on his side. Sale of cigarettes was prohibited in Iowa for 25 years, from 1896 to 1921.

Some 1930s women insisted as a matter of personal right that they be able to smoke when and where they wanted. A Mrs. Taylor Scott Hardin of unknown address sent a clipping to the *Marshalltown Times-Republican* telling of a group of women defiantly smoking as they paraded down Fifth Avenue in New York.

Mrs. Hardin said the purpose of the parade was to "quash a ridiculous taboo." She called the cigarette "the torch of freedom." Tongue in cheek, *Times-Republican* editor Frank Moscrip replied that women did have the right to smoke, or to chew tobacco if they wanted to, or even to scratch a match where many a male smoker of the times did, on the seat of his pants.

Now that smoking has been proved a major health hazard how ironic it is that women once fought so hard to gain acceptance as smokers.

But maybe the greatest paradox of all in church-oriented Iowa showed up in so-called liquor control.

Iowa law forbade the manufacture and sale of alcoholic beverages anywhere in the state beginning in 1916. National prohibition went into effect in 1920. Both laws were still on the books in 1931. There were no legal beer joints, no legal bars or liquor stores, no lawful place where you could buy a bottle or glass.

Liquor and beer ads were absent from newspapers and radio. (There was no TV.) Famous sports figures did not extol the qualities of certain beers on the air waves. Alcohol sponsors did not select the outstanding players in Big Ten and other athletic contests.

But there was bootlegging; ah, yes, there was bootlegging! Selling unlawful liquor was a major business almost everywhere in Iowa (as in the rest of the nation). Some of the liquor was moonshine whisky, wine, gin, home brew beer. Most was raw alcohol.

Speakeasies (taverns, usually with doors locked) sold drinks over the bar, law or no law. Fraternal clubs like the Elks and Eagles did the same thing. Country clubs and veterans clubs did too. Out on the dark streets and in alleys, and at back doors, bootleggers sold small bottles to furtive buyers.

At first the demand was great, supplies limited. Buyers had to pay as much as $16 or $17, even up to $25, for a gallon of alky if they wanted that much. Competition stiffened and the price slid to $5 a gallon. If you were going to a party or dance, however, you usually got half a pint that fit in your back pocket from a bootlegger. Cost, $1.50.

Iowa's favorite alcoholic drink was "spiked beer." It consisted of a bottle of virtually nonalcoholic beer fortified by filling up the neck of the bottle with alky. The next step was to put your thumb over the opening and turn the bottle upside down to mix the alky with the beer. There was reason to believe that "spiking beer" originated in Iowa and spread to other Midwest states.

Much of the alcohol was brought into Iowa by rum-runners from Chicago, where Gangster Al ("Scarface") Capone held murderous sway in the trade. But Iowa moonshiners made a lot of it too, in caves, basements, woods, hog houses, and farms.

German farmers operating their own stills built a thriving business in bootleg rye whisky around Templeton in Carroll County, Iowa. "Templeton rye" had a market as far away as New York City.

Those Templeton farmers were a pain in the neck to federal enforcement agents. They couldn't catch the culprits. Under federal rules, the agents had to take along a local officer such as Carroll Sheriff Frank Bucheit on each raid. Bucheit was not a good choice. He was "in" with the farmers. He wasn't going to let them get caught.

The feds came in one day in a hurry, grabbed Bucheit and sped out into the country. The first farmer came to the door all dusty and breathing hard. "Jesus Christ, Frank," he complained, "you don't give a guy much notice any more." Again, no results.

Liquor-law breaking became so rampant around the state and nation, real or imagined corruption of public officials so common and gangster violence so widespread that prohibition collapsed. It was repealed in 1933 at both the federal and state levels. Even "Bible Belt" Iowa surprisingly gave a majority vote for repeal in a referendum. That may have been, in part at least, because some voters personally opposed to liquor decided it would be best to get rid of an unenforceable law.

There was no doubt that plenty of bootlegging took place in old-time strait-laced Iowa. But it may not have been as much as it appeared. Liquor raids, liquor seizures, trials, convictions and the like were big news regularly, often on the front page. Peaceable events of the times rarely were given big coverage.

When the dust settled in the mid-1930s, Iowa still had restrictive liquor laws. Sale of hard liquor by the drink was forbidden. The only legal way to buy the stuff was by the bottle in a state-operated liquor store. (Beer, however, did become readily available in food stores and elsewhere.)

Anyway, between the 1930s and 1990s, Iowa moved well away not only from its anti-gambling and traditional personal moral standards, but to a wide-open level in liquor as well. It became easy to buy it in all kinds of business establishments, including food stores. Bottles of whisky showed up near the corn flakes and brandy not far from the cookies on grocery shelves. It was not uncommon to see a customer at a checkout counter with a carton of milk along with a jug of vodka. Commercials extolling brands of beer took over television screens. Newspapers and magazines carried hard liquor ads without hindrance. Deep changes beyond the grasp of bygone Iowa.

Wherein lies responsibility for the monumental changes in Iowa decorum the last 60 years plus?

A Warren County minister believes a long decline in church influence is a major factor. "A high percentage of people indicate in the polls that they believe in God," said the Reverend George Blakesley III, pastor of the Scotch Ridge Presbyterian Church, "but the church is not a center of family life that it used to be."

He expressed belief the people have become suspect of institutions, and the church has suffered as a result. He added that the "baby boomers" born in the late 1940s and 1950s originally moved away from the church in substantial numbers. He thinks they are returning because "they want that foundation for their children."

Another minister, the Reverend Robert L. Brunk of the Church of Christ in Bayard, Iowa, reacted angrily some years ago to an ad in the *Register.* The ad said: "Des Moines has a WHOREHOUSE in it. For a good time call 274-4686." The ad was placed by a Des Moines theater presenting a musical entitled *The Best Little Whorehouse in Texas.*

In a letter to the *Register,* Mr. Brunk exclaimed: "I think I liked the Iowa of my youth better. Iowa, my Iowa, where have you gone!"

I·O·W·A
HERITAGE
COLLECTION

An ever-expanding series of original books and classic reprints about Iowa, selected for insightful portrayals of the state and its people.